Soviet Leadership in Transition

Jerry F. Hough
Soviet Leadership in Transition

The Brookings Institution
Washington, D.C.

Library of Congress Cataloging in Publication Data:

Hough, Jerry F   1935–
Soviet leadership in transition.

Includes bibliographical references and index.
1. Russia—Politics and government—1953–
I. Title.
DK274.H68   947.085   80-67873
ISBN 0-8157-3742-4
ISBN 0-8157-3741-6 (pbk.)

9 8 7 6 5 4 3 2 1

THE BROOKINGS INSTITUTION is an independent organization devoted to nonpartisan research, education, and publication in economics, government, foreign policy, and the social sciences generally. Its principal purposes are to aid in the development of sound public policies and to promote public understanding of issues of national importance.

The Institution was founded on December 8, 1927, to merge the activities of the Institute for Government Research, founded in 1916, the Institute of Economics, founded in 1922, and the Robert Brookings Graduate School of Economics and Government, founded in 1924.

The Board of Trustees is responsible for the general administration of the Institution, while the immediate direction of the policies, program, and staff is vested in the President, assisted by an advisory committee of the officers and staff. The by-laws of the Institution state: "It is the function of the Trustees to make possible the conduct of scientific research, and publication, under the most favorable conditions, and to safeguard the independence of the research staff in the pursuit of their studies and in the publication of the results of such studies. It is not a part of their function to determine, control, or influence the conduct of particular investigations or the conclusions reached."

The President bears final responsibility for the decision to publish a manuscript as a Brookings book. In reaching his judgment on the competence, accuracy, and objectivity of each study, the President is advised by the director of the appropriate research program and weighs the views of a panel of expert outside readers who report to him in confidence on the quality of the work. Publication of a work signifies that it is deemed a competent treatment worthy of public consideration but does not imply endorsement of conclusions or recommendations.

The Institution maintains its position of neutrality on issues of public policy in order to safeguard the intellectual freedom of the staff. Hence interpretations or conclusions in Brookings publications should be understood to be solely those of the authors and should not be attributed to the Institution, to it trustees, officers, or other staff members, or to the organizations that support its research.

Foreword

The present leaders of the Soviet Union, Leonid Brezhnev and his associates, are the last of that group of men who were promoted precipitously in the wake of Stalin's Great Purge of 1937–38. They have therefore been at the top for more than forty years. No other country has a defense minister who became a member of the cabinet as long ago as 1941, or a foreign minister who was named ambassador to Washington during World War II.

Precisely who will succeed whom in the top levels of the Soviet government is of course unpredictable, but those who will dominate the government and Communist party in the 1980s already hold middle-level political and administrative jobs. They are men who differ radically from the present leaders in background, education, and experience.

In this book Jerry F. Hough, professor of political science and policy science at Duke University, analyzes these generational differences and examines the generational changes occurring within the various Soviet hierarchies—the central and provincial political and administrative structures, the military, and the foreign policy establishment. Many of the data he presents have hitherto been unavailable in the West.

In the last two chapters Hough assesses the ways in which the impending succession may affect Soviet economic reform and Soviet-American relations. He argues that the most important choice the Soviet Union will have to make in the 1980s is that between seeking military superiority or economic parity in relation to the West. This policy choice—and others—will be made by the new Soviet leaders, but Hough believes that Western actions will be influential. He concludes by suggesting how the United States might try to improve relations as the Soviet leadership changes.

The author conducted most of the research for this book at the Historical Library of the RSFSR in Moscow and at the Australian National Library in Canberra. He is grateful to the staffs of these libraries, and especially to Nina Rodionova, for their unfailing courtesy and helpfulness.

The following persons read drafts of chapters and made valuable comments: Sheila Fitzpatrick, Raymond Garthoff, Franklyn Griffiths, T. H. Rigby, John D. Steinbruner, and S. Frederick Starr. As the footnotes only partially suggest, the contribution of the author's wife, Sheila Fitzpatrick, was especially important. Her knowledge of events in the Soviet Union during the 1920s and 1930s shaped his understanding of the formative experiences of the present Soviet elite.

The research for chapter 6 was in large part supported by grants from the Institute of World Politics and the Russian Institute of Columbia University. The work in Canberra was made possible by a grant from the Australian National University. The author's views are his own and should not be ascribed to any of the persons or institutions whose help has been acknowledged here or to the trustees, officers, or other staff members of the Brookings Institution.

BRUCE K. MACLAURY
President

May 1980
Washington, D.C.

Contents

Tables

Figures

1

Problems of the 1980s

THE 1980s have begun with a crisis in Soviet-American relations. The Soviet invasion of Afghanistan has spread alarm throughout the United States, where nerves were already on edge from its defeat in Vietnam, the threats to inexpensive petroleum, and the seizure of its hostages in Iran. Many have begun to talk—some with great fear but others almost with relish—about an open return to the tension and confrontations of the cold war.

Yet in a fundamental sense there can never be a return to the cold war of the 1940s and 1950s. It was a very different time. The Soviet Union was still a developing nation, its economy in shambles from World War II and the aftermath of collectivization. The American government could conduct foreign policy without being seriously concerned over the possible destruction of its homeland, and it alone was in a position to use military power in the third world. Indeed, the rigidities of his dogmas led Joseph Stalin to reject the idea of supporting such men as Nehru, Sukarno, and Mossadegh, for he saw them as agents of American capitalism.

The situation today is very different: the establishment of near-equality in military power between the United States and the Soviet Union has transformed their political relationship. Now the United States is thirty minutes from devastation, and the Soviet Union is acquiring a mobile limited-war capability. Worst of all, the potential centers of conflict are not Berlin and South Korea, which had only politico-ideological significance for the superpowers, but the oil fields of the Middle East at a time of energy crisis in both countries. Not only is this area of far more vital interest to each side, but it does not have the internal political stability that Berlin and South Korea had thirty years ago. Furthermore, the Soviet Union has long since abandoned its reluctance to cooperate with and assist indigenous non-Communist forces in the third world.

The problems today are thus more complicated and dangerous than they were in the 1940s and the 1950s. At a time when a political convulsion occurs in some third world country almost every year, both the United States and the USSR have tended to become fearful that their political positions are being eroded by forces over which they have no control—but which are perhaps being controlled or at least provoked by the other side. Now that the lead time on the development of new weapons and on weapon manufacture has become so long, policymakers must judge not only what will be necessary to maintain the military balance next year but what will be needed five or ten years in the future. Each country has a natural tendency to be profoundly suspicious of the intentions of the other. Since a leadership change is imminent in the Soviet Union, and the United States—and Western Europe—seems to be moving in a conservative, anti-Soviet direction, each side is worried that changes in the other will make the future even more dangerous than the present. All of this increase in anxiety is taking place at a time when the achievement of general military parity makes the possibility of military escalation on both sides much greater than it was in the past.

The result is paradoxical. On the one hand, the serious economic problems in both the Soviet Union and the United States—especially those associated with the energy crisis—demand wholehearted efforts to reduce the cost of the military and its consumption of petroleum and, indeed, cooperation in increasing the production of petroleum and other energy sources throughout the world. On the other hand, the tensions that are exacerbated by the energy crisis lead to increased military consumption of energy and a decline in economic cooperation in the development of energy; they therefore create greater shortages and stronger reasons for military actions to relieve them.

In these circumstances, managing the Soviet-American conflict, let alone moving toward arms control, is a complicated task. Each side must be concerned about the intentions as well as the capabilities of the other. Each must be sensitive to the anxieties produced by the newly created military balance and the energy crisis, and each must be skillful in its use of gestures to reassure some of the most worried groups on the other side.

Unfortunately, the policies of both the United States and the Soviet Union have left much to be desired in this regard. Even before its ill-advised invasion of Afghanistan, the USSR had acted foolishly in the way it built its strategic rocket force. Whether the Soviet leaders had the ultimate goal of establishing equality with the United States or superiority over it, they took steps early in the deployment process (for example, in the number of rockets they installed and their throw weight) that were guaranteed to increase fears in the United States and stimulate the development of new American weapon systems.

The United States, for its part, has been ungenerous about giving the Soviet Union the kinds of symbolic acknowledgment of equality for which the USSR has an almost pathological yearning. We have gone out of our way to take actions that were certain to offend the Soviet Union without inhibiting it from taking action or without even changing its cost-benefit calculations. We have been vigorous in punishing the Soviet Union for actions it has already taken, but lax in setting up a system of incentives and potential penalties that might constrain Soviet behavior in the future. For example, we forswore the use of the grain weapon before the invasion of Afghanistan, when it might have served as a deterrent to Soviet action, but then used it afterward.

American Perceptions

One important reason that neither the Soviet Union nor the United States has created a network of incentives and penalties that would promote smoother relations between them is that neither has a sound understanding of the political system of the other. We are all familiar with the dogmatic concept of "American imperialism" that has crippled the conduct of Soviet foreign policy in the past—and to a certain extent even today—but we are less aware of the existence of a similar problem in the United States.

A quarter century ago, our image of the Soviet Union was summarized in the concept of "totalitarianism," and the language of some of the best scholarly work treated this abstraction almost as a living thing:

Totalitarianism . . . subverts the direct restraints immediately after the seizure of power but, unlike traditional dictatorships, it proceeds, once entrenched, to pulverize all existing associations in society in order to remake that society and subsequently even man himself, according to certain "ideal" conceptions. In time it even attempts, not always successfully, to overcome the natural restraints on political power. Without doing so, totalitarianism can never achieve the isolation of the individual and the mass monolithic homogeneity that are its aim. Only with both of them (the paradox between them is more apparent than real) can the existing pluralism be transformed into an active unanimity of the entire population which will make the transformation of society, and ultimately man, possible.[1]

The essence of the totalitarian model was the assumption that the Soviet leaders were imbued with a relentless drive for power, either for its own sake or as a means to the end of transforming society. In either case the implications for our image of Soviet foreign policy were clear. One might concede that the Soviet Union was cautious in the actual conduct of its foreign policy at a particular time, but ultimately the relentless drive of totalitarianism for power and for a transformation of man and society had no reason to stop at a national border.

During the last twenty-five years our more simplistic images of the adversary have been eroded. Nikita Khrushchev's limitations on the arbitrary power of the secret police eliminated one of the main features of totalitarianism as we had seen it, and, however one wants to characterize Leonid I. Brezhnev and Aleksei N. Kosygin, the two post-Khrushchev leaders have scarcely been ruthless transformers of society in their policies. As a result, few scholars today think that the totalitarian model is an accurate summary of the contemporary Soviet Union, and many will not even use the word *totalitarian* in labeling the USSR. (*Authoritarian,* which denotes a more conservative and limited repressive regime, is the word more often used.)

For a series of reasons, however, the United States has had great difficulty in developing a more sophisticated and discriminating understanding of Soviet motivations and of the inner workings of the Soviet system. Unlike the Soviet Union, we do not have 500 to 1,000 specialists studying the contemporary situation inside the adversary country, and our foreign correspondents are not career internationalists who have mastered the Russian language. The U.S. academic community has tended to focus on a study of the past, whereas the specialists in the government, except the economists, have concentrated on the analysis of current news developments and virtually unknowable details about the political positions and loyalties of Politburo members. The Soviet Union has encouraged this development by following an unfortunate censorship policy that permits us to read about most of the

1. Zbigniew Brzezinski, "Totalitarianism and Rationality," *American Political Science Review*, vol. 50 (September 1956), p. 753.

defects in Soviet society but not much about those aspects of the political system that correspond most closely to our idea of democracy.

As a result, the Soviet system in large part remains an abstraction to us. If we no longer see an active totalitarianism transforming society, we now talk of a dead or dying one—of a petrified or ossified system. If we no longer believe that the leadership serves as the instrument of a dynamic ideology, we may now speak as if it were the automatic representative of some other force, such as Russian national character, the Russian historical tradition, Russian political culture, or, of course, the bureaucracy.

In the most popular of these views, it is the bureaucracy that rules in the Soviet Union, a bureaucracy that opposes any significant change— except, perhaps, in the direction of tighter discipline on the general public, greater privileges for the bureaucrats, and a more nationalistic posture toward the West as justification for the public sacrifices at home. But, it is believed, even this change in posture would be accepted by bureaucrats only as a last resort, lest it interfere with their cherished desire to travel abroad and buy Western goods.

Our popular thinking does not, however, reflect the realities. In little more than a century the Soviet Union has evolved from a traditional underdeveloped country, with most of its population in serfdom, into a leading industrial power. (As late as 1930 the basic Soviet social and economic indicators were showing roughly the same level of development as Mexico or Egypt had reached in the early 1970s.) Since World War I its elite has changed radically several times. From 1917 to 1921 Russia underwent a social revolution that eliminated the old tsarist elite, replacing it with the generation of Communist politicians and administrators who had joined the party before the revolution. Members of that generation largely disappeared from the scene during the Great Purge of the late 1930s (except at the Politburo level), and in turn the generation that came into prominence at that time is now represented by only a few men at the very top. In the past twenty-five years a rigid and dogmatic world view has been subjected to repeated attack as Soviet scholars, encouraged by the leadership, have developed a more realistic understanding of the world. It therefore seems unlikely that the Soviet Union of the 1980s can be understood simply in terms of the forces and values that shaped Russian actions in the 1880s or even in the 1940s.

Similarly, it must be a gross oversimplification to see the Soviet bureaucracy as an undifferentiated opponent of change. In the modern world most people work for some kind of bureaucracy. If they have made progress in their careers, they usually have some administrative authority over other people and are therefore bureaucrats themselves. In the Soviet Union, as elsewhere, bureaucrats are not just limited to top ministerial officials, but include factory directors and shop heads, almost all army officers, school principals, trade union officials, heads of scientific institutes and laboratories, managers of hospitals and their wards, and so forth. Since so many people are bureaucrats, they certainly cannot all have identical personalities and political attitudes. The same is true of the party members within the bureaucracy. Approximately 21 percent of Soviet men between the ages of thirty and sixty are members of the Communist party—and some 50 percent of men of that age with a college education. No party to which such a large proportion of the population belongs can be a selfless, unified priesthood.[2]

In particular, whatever their attitudes toward certain fundamentals of the system, the officials of the Soviet bureaucracy cannot be single-minded opponents of change on current policy questions. American historians working on tsarist Russia have been moving away from a study of the socialist dissidents of the time and have begun looking seriously at the politics of the tsarist bureaucracy. They have discovered that the old view of a dichotomy between the progressive intelligentsia and the conservative bureaucracy was largely a myth. The bureaucracy itself contained progressives as well as conservatives. It had proposed many of the reforms that the tsar carried out, and many of its officials had pushed for other reforms that were not enacted. The Soviet bureaucracy is no different. Although, like any bureaucracy, it contains officials who can be counted upon to oppose any reform that is contrary to their interests, it also has administrators who publish articles favoring some reform. Behind the scenes there are even more spirited fights for policy alternatives.

But who are these men and women who run the country?[3] They are

2. Jerry F. Hough, *The Soviet Union and Social Science Theory* (Harvard University Press, 1977), pp. 129–31.

3. In general, in this book I shall be speaking only about men. Women occupy a number of middle-level positions—especially in health, education, and culture—but there are at present no women among the Central Committee secretaries and department heads, members of the Council of Ministers, or regional first secretaries.

of course the members of the "New Class" that Milovan Djilas has discussed, and they are the people who receive the privileges that Hedrick Smith and Robert Kaiser have described.[4] Nevertheless, they remain a great faceless unknown to us. Although we recognize the dissidents as real people, we have almost no understanding of the bureaucrats, the people belonging to the Soviet middle class or upper-middle class. What changes are taking place among them? How is their thinking changing? What policy dilemmas do they face? These are the questions to which this book is dedicated, for unless we begin to acquire some knowledge about the most influential class in the Soviet Union, we shall have little chance of managing our difficult relationship with that country with any degree of sophistication.

Generational Change in the Bureaucracy

Since the Soviet system is, in Alfred Meyer's words, a "bureaucracy writ large,"[5] a comprehensive study of Soviet officialdom would require many volumes, each dealing with the officials of an institution or profession, each describing not only their sociological characteristics but also the range of their views and the debates and political conflicts in which they are engaged. It would attempt to show the variations among officials of different nationalities within these institutions or professions. Unfortunately, even if the reader had the patience for such a study, the West has simply not reached the stage of research at which it could be written. The very idea of meaningful political participation by Soviet citizens—even those of the upper-middle class—is still so controversial that Western scholars are just beginning to investigate the published debates and open political struggles that abound in the Soviet media. It will be years before they have accumulated enough books and articles to make the kind of sound summary statements that are needed.

This book is, therefore, a preliminary effort. To some extent I try to look at the institutional framework within which the Soviet upper-mid-

4. Milovan Djilas, *The New Class: An Analysis of the Communist System* (Praeger, 1957); Hedrick Smith, *The Russians* (Quadrangle, 1976); Robert G. Kaiser, *Russia: The People and the Power* (Atheneum, 1976).
5. Alfred G. Meyer, *The Soviet Political System: An Interpretation* (Random House, 1965), p. 458.

dle class functions, as well as at the basic interests of the different institutions in relation to the impending Soviet policy dilemmas. But essentially I concentrate on one facet of reality—the movement of several generations of officials with very different life experiences through
the upper levels of the administrative and political hierarchies.

Instinctively, Americans tend not to pay much attention to the generational factor in their analysis of higher elite politics in the United
States. Rightly or wrongly, no one comments on the fact that the last
decade has seen the generation that bore the brunt of World War II
combat move into the top leadership posts. Although the differences in
age between Ronald Reagan, Jimmy Carter, and Edward Kennedy are
often noted, few perceive these men as incorporating generational attitudes of any importance.

In the Soviet Union, by contrast, people are quite conscious of generations and refer to them repeatedly both in print and in private conversations. Perhaps because the events in Russia in the twentieth century had dramatic effects, and because the experiences of different age
groups have been very diverse, people may just assume that generational differences are important. However, generations are mentioned
so frequently and in such widely varying contexts that it is difficult to
avoid the conclusion that the generalizations being made are based on
observations of real variations in attitudes and behavior. Certainly Soviet scholars often testify privately about the importance of the generational factor in explaining attitudes within their own fields.

Whatever the actual situation today, the Soviet Union in the 1920s,
the 1930s, and the 1940s certainly passed through a series of cataclys-
mic events, notably rapid industrialization and collectivization, the
Great Purge, and World War II. These events had a tremendous impact not only on the elite of the time but also on teenagers and young
adults, for they were accompanied by major changes in the educational
system through which the latter were passing.

The dramatic differences in life opportunities produced by these
events have had a number of direct and indirect echo effects as members of the various generations have aged and begun to rise through the
political and administrative hierarchies. Although the events of their
youth may conceivably have affected their life-long views (that is, as
the views of Americans who will be in their forties and fifties in the late

Table 1-1. *Period of Birth of New RSFSR Regional First Secretaries and U.S. State Governors, and Their Immediate Predecessors, 1969–78*

Period of birth	Number of secretaries	Number of governors
1901–08	0	1
1909–16	27	18
1917–24	14	35
1925–32	27	28
1933–40	0	15
1941–48	0	1

Sources: For the Russian Republic: *Deputaty Verkhovnogo Soveta SSSR* for the 7th, 8th, and 9th convocations of the Supreme Soviet (Moscow: Izdatel'stvo "Izvestiia Sovetov Deputatov Trudiashchikhsia SSSR," 1966, 1970, and 1974); and the 1966, 1972, and 1977 editions of the *Ezhegodnik bol'shoi sovetskoi entsiklopedii* (Moscow: Izdatel'stvo "Sovetskaia Entsiklopediia"). For the United States: *Information Please Almanac, 1979* (Viking, 1978), p. 702; *Congress and the Nation* (Congressional Quarterly Service, 1977), vol. 4, *1973-76*, pp.39-45; and various editions of *Who's Who in America*.

1990s may be abnormally affected by Vietnam), these events were more important in that they determined the type of person who was promoted, the type of training the various generations received, and even how each generation is perceived by others.

Two facts about generations are especially crucial for an understanding of Soviet reality in the 1970s and 1980s. First, over one-half of the Politburo voting members come from among those who were thrust upward after the Great Purge, when they were in their thirties, and who have been in high posts for forty years. Second, the enormous impact of World War II on the education of the youth of the time has been strongly felt in the middle levels of the bureaucracy in recent years.

In particular, the generation of an age to have borne the brunt of the war was in its fifties during the 1970s and therefore should have been the main source for middle-level recruitment at that time. If, however, one looks at the pattern of replacement of regional party first secretaries in the huge Russian Soviet Federated Socialist Republic (RSFSR) over the last decade, one finds that the new first secretaries were born thirteen years later on the average than their immediate predecessors, as against only a four-year age difference between newly elected American state governors and their predecessors. The dates of birth of the predecessors and successors among the American governors are distributed along a fairly normal curve, but among the

RSFSR secretaries these dates give clear evidence of a missing generation (see table 1-1).

The pool of men entering their fifties in the late 1970s and early 1980s and hence ready for promotion to the top levels is different in size and in level of education from the pool of men who entered their fifties in the previous decade. In 1960 there were 17,800,000 men who had been born between 1924 and 1933, as against 8,850,000 who had been born between 1915 and 1924, and, to repeat, the difference in the number of well-educated men was much greater. As will be discussed in later chapters, there has been no inhibition against moving members of the postwar generation (essentially those born after 1925) into key posts at middle levels of the bureaucracy, and they have had ample experience for further promotion if a Soviet leader decides to undertake a rejuvenation of the central party and government apparatus.

Soviet Policy Dilemmas

Of course, if the Soviet system has indeed petrified, it is irrelevant that a large number of better-educated officials are just entering their fifties. Either the older leaders will keep them from key positions for years, or the younger leaders will simply represent the same traditional bureaucratic interests as their predecessors, so that their rise to the top will change nothing.

The thesis of petrification is, however, one that we should be seeking evidence for, instead of accepting dogmatically. In the first place, it is possible that the next general secretary will have a different set of assumptions from Brezhnev about the most advantageous personnel policy to follow. Since Brezhnev has permitted no logical successor to arise, many must see themselves as the appropriate general secretary, either immediately or in the relatively short run. Thus any new leader may feel compelled to move against potential rivals. He may also fear that the administrative elite is becoming so encrusted that it threatens economic performance, and that he must face the danger of challenging the Central Committee of the Communist Party of the Soviet Union to avoid greater potential dangers in the streets.

In the second place, it would be extraordinary if nothing changes in the Soviet Union over the next five years, for as the Soviet Union enters the 1980s, it confronts a set of interrelated problems as complex as the ones it had to deal with after the deaths of Lenin and Stalin. In a November 1978 speech to the Central Committee, Brezhnev said that the economic problems were great enough to threaten political stability,[6] and these problems promise to worsen in the face of an impending energy shortage and a large drop in the number of people entering the labor force in the 1980s. At the same time, the achievement of rough military parity with the West successfully caps a fifty-year program that has been one of the strongest motivating and legitimating drives within the Soviet system. But this achievement raises to the forefront the question of what to do now: to seek to push forward for superiority and use it for political gains or to reduce the priority given to the military for so many decades.

In the political realm, too, many problems are arising. An imbalance in the birthrates of non-Russians and Russians requires either a shift of investment into non-Russian areas or the encouragement of non-Slavs to move into the Russian Republic, with all the possible accompanying social problems. This decision must be made at a time when the radical Islamic movements south of the Soviet Union have sent shock waves of anxiety through the more-educated Moscow circles—and perhaps through the population as a whole.

Other political questions lurk just beneath the surface. It is not certain whether the political mechanisms that proved successful in the period of rapid industrialization will work as effectively now that the economy and the society have changed. Does the enormous rise in the educational level of the Soviet population over the last few decades require changes in party methods if political control and work effectiveness are to be maintained? Is there not some way to secure a more regular renewal of leadership without incurring the threat either of a loss of central control or of dominance by a single leader?

It is, however, the economic question that is central to all the decisions to be made. Many Westerners have talked for years about Soviet economic difficulties and crises, but for the first time since the immediate post-Stalin period the broad Soviet public, as well as the bureaucracy and intelligentsia, has recognized the need for some type of major economic change. One highly placed Soviet intellectual privately re-

6. *Pravda*, November 28, 1978, pp. 1–2.

ports that the 1978 Brezhnev speech was a veritable bombshell, and it is certainly true that during 1979 the Soviet press published innumerable articles discussing improvement in the economic mechanism.

But to say that economic change is necessary is not to say what that change should be. One instinctive answer is to plan more rigorously, to tighten controls, to be more ruthless in punishing those who do not produce. Besides the top-level reluctance to dismiss ministers, legal and trade union protections often make it difficult to fire people at lower levels. The belief that this leads to excessive laziness and irresponsibility is pervasive. In practice, it was such a tightening of discipline that Brezhnev demanded in his 1979 speech to the Central Committee, but except for a rather general Central Committee decree,[7] his words have not yet been matched by deeds.

The less instinctive answer to the economic difficulties—especially for a Marxist-Leninist—is to reduce the level of detailed planning, to rely more heavily on economic incentives, and to decentralize more decisions to the plant level. Although this should result in the imposition of even greater discipline on those who do not meet market standards, the problem of combining governmental regulations and market mechanisms in a way that controls the major economic producers without fettering them has obviously not been completely solved in the West. In particular, there is quite a widespread fear in the Soviet Union that managers will not really be controlled by some "invisible hand" but will fullfill any profitability goals by simply raising prices. Therefore a policy of decentralizing decisionmaking authority and of using market mechanisms more fully is only the first step in deciding precisely how that policy should be carried out.

The problems inherent in defining an economic reform that works effectively are intensified by the fact that reform is related to all the other problems of Soviet society. On the one hand, the intensification of central controls means even less autonomy for the non-Russian republics and even more resentment on this score. Greater controls on the individual, coupled with a reduction in contact with the West and its goods and culture, run the danger of being much less tolerable to the present educated public than to earlier generations. The dangers become particularly great if the tightening of controls does not work economically—if the economy has simply become too complex

7. Ibid., November 28, 1979, pp. 1–2, and January 12, 1980, p. 1.

to be planned more intensively from the center and if an aggressive policy toward the West results in an arms race that puts increased pressure on consumption.

On the other hand, the adjustments in prices and wages that would be required by even a partial movement in the direction of market socialism could also pose a political problem (for example, if the price of meat in the state stores were doubled). A transfer of funds from the military to consumption would alleviate that problem, and the labor shortage would also be helped by a reduction in the size of the army. Greater integration of the Soviet economy into the world market would provide strong competitive forces to improve quality; greater availability of Western goods and the opportunity to travel abroad would increase the incentive to produce more in order to earn more. But more contact with the outside world and more decentralization of decision-making authority to lower levels would at a minimum raise fears that political control over the non-Russians—and perhaps even the Russians—would be endangered.

Unfortunately, at the time when these serious economic, political, and social problems have converged, the ruling Party Politburo continues to be dominated by members of a unique generation that has been near the top for forty years. Because the Great Purge of 1937-38 thrust upward many men who were in their thirties, leaders who today are in their seventies can have had incredible tenures.

Such political longevity is certainly found among the core members of the Politburo of early 1980. Brezhnev and his leading deputy, Andrei P. Kirilenko, were regional party secretaries before World War II. The chairman of the Council of Ministers, Aleksei Kosygin, and the minister of defense, Dmitrii F. Ustinov, were USSR people's commissars (ministers) of light industry and the defense industry, respectively, at that time. Mikhail A. Suslov was a regional first secretary (the closest Soviet equivalent to an American state governor) in 1939 and has held the post of Central Committee secretary since 1946. Andrei A. Gromyko, the minister of foreign affairs, was head of the American desk of the People's Commissariat of Foreign Affairs in 1939 and ambassador to the United States in 1943. Boris N. Ponomarev, Central Committee secretary and head of the international department of the Central Committee, was named to the executive committee of the Comintern in 1936. (President Carter was twelve years old then, and Senator Kennedy was four.) Even if those who replace these men are not much younger, the length of time that they will have been near the top will almost surely have been much shorter, for the Soviet promotion patterns after the 1937-38 purge were more normal by Western standards.

In short, the Politburo continues to be dominated by men who have been accustomed all their adult lives to one set of problems: the need to build the primary industrial base, the need to catch up militarily with a more powerful West, and the need to raise the educational and cultural level of a vast population. Until the mid-1970s the Brezhnev regime functioned fairly well, even though his "administration" was labeled a "government of clerks" when it came into power in 1964 and was accused of petrification soon after.[8] Steady growth both in living standards and military power was achieved, and, despite Western predictions of nationality difficulties and even riots in the streets in the 1970s, the country has been remarkably stable.

In the last five years, however, the Brezhnev regime has shown signs of loss of vigor. Ministers are repeatedly criticized and not removed; posts (for example, the chairmanship of the national Trade Union Council) can remain unfilled for up to eighteen months; the last three additions to the Politburo voting membership have been personal associates of Brezhnev for twenty to forty years, one of them (Konstantin Chernenko) having been his personal secretary. In the policy realm, very few, if any, hard decisions were taken in the second half of the 1970s. Characteristically, Brezhnev's bombshell speech of November 1978 was followed seven months later by a Central Committee and Council of Ministers decision on economic management that simply reaffirmed the need for greater economic incentives, more local initiative, and stronger central control—that is, that changed nothing.[9] Now in their seventies the old leaders face a new set of problems, but they give no indication of having the ability to adjust their priorities or at least of having the energy to cope with the interrelated decisions that change would require.

8. Zbigniew Brzezinski, "A Government of Clerks: What Khrushchev's Ouster Means," *New Republic*, November 14, 1964, pp. 15–18; Robert Conquest, "Immobilism and Decay," *Problems of Communism*, vol. 15 (September–October 1966), pp. 35–37; Zbigniew Brzezinski, "Reflections on the Soviet System," *Problems of Communism*, vol. 17 (May–June 1968), pp. 44–48.

9. *Ekonomicheskaia gazeta*, no. 32 (August 1979), special supplement.

It is of course not unusual for a leader, a reign, or an administration to become tired after a number of years in office, especially when illness occurs. It is not unusual for problems to pile up. What would be unusual would be for a new leader or administration not to try to make its mark on history by attempting to resolve some of them. What would be unusual would be for a generation of officials with such different experiences from their predecessors to have the same perspectives on these policy dilemmas—especially in regard to the desirability of neglecting them. The generational change that I am talking about is not a trivial one. The generations that are leaving the scene are those who were most deprived of contact with the West until middle age, the ones whose work careers spanned much of the worst period of the Stalin era. Many of their members (particularly those of the Brezhnev generation) have good reason to be nervous about a thorough discussion of 1937 and 1938, the years of the Great Purge.

Men born in 1927 or 1928, on the other hand, had hardly begun their careers by the time of Stalin's death in 1953. They had the freer access to information of the post-Stalin period before their minds had been set, and, in fact, they were young enough to be truly shocked by Khrushchev's revelations about Stalin. Indeed, those who have since been successful were part of the drive to break up the rigidities of Stalinist doctrine in the 1950s and the 1960s. Those who deal with the international world in their professions received exposure to the West very early in their careers and repeatedly thereafter.

Although it would be wrong to proclaim the certainty of change, it would be even more incorrect to deny its possibility. In any case the time has come for Americans to give more serious attention to the people who are rising through the various Soviet hierarchies. It is only when we can begin to see that the Soviet system is staffed by real people with real hopes and fears and values and interests—and changing ones over time—that we will be in a position to break away from our old abstractions and manage our relationship with that country in a subtle and sophisticated way.

2

The Changing Soviet People

ALTHOUGH this book focuses upon the Soviet political and administrative elite—a fairly narrow group consisting essentially of those who have reached middle age and who have risen to quite high managerial levels—it should never be forgotten that the elite functions within a broader framework. As the collapse of the shah's regime in Iran illustrated, the instruments of control—the army, the police, and so forth— upon which a repressive government must rely are composed of real people, and these instruments can dissolve. Regimes can conduct unpopular policies and survive, but there comes a time—for reasons that are poorly understood by scholars—when their "legitimacy" is stretched to the breaking point. A political elite that wants to survive must strive to prevent the development of too great a sense of alienation among politically-relevant segments of the population.

Americans often talk as if these problems of popular support did not exist in a Communist regime because of the presence of some superhuman totalitarian control. This is simply wrong. The Hungarian army collapsed in 1956 and the regime with it; only Khrushchev's use of the Soviet army reestablished the government. Today it seems clear that the Polish army and police could not keep the Communist system in power if it were not for the threat of Soviet intervention. The fact that the instruments of control in the Soviet Union have functioned so much more effectively over the years indicates that at some level the party has maintained the support of large segments of the population.

Yet values can change over time, especially with the development of industrialization and a rise in the educational level within a country, and these changes can have profound political consequences. For example, hereditary monarchy as a form of government seemed compatible with preindustrial populations but has proved unsuccessful in industrial nations. The question is, over the long run, will authoritarian Communist political systems be more durable in the face of industrialization?

That is a question on which there is still little empirical evidence, and of course only the future will furnish a definitive answer to it. Nevertheless, it deserves careful consideration. As W.W. Rostow observed, Communist regimes have been a "disease of the transition."[1] Communist revolutions based on internal forces (that is, those in Russia, China, Cuba, Vietnam, and Yugoslavia) have not occurred in advanced industrial countries as Marx had predicted, but in countries in early stages of industrialization. Russia, for example, was 80 percent rural in 1917, with half its population illiterate, and the peasantry little more than fifty years from serfdom. Even so, it was considerably more advanced economically than the other countries that have had successful Communist revolutions. Today in the third world, the revolutions that seem the most radical are occurring in underdeveloped countries like Yemen, Ethiopia, and Afghanistan rather than in industrially more advanced ones like India and Brazil.

The pattern of successful Communist revolutions has been so consistent that it cannot have been accidental. There must be something in the Leninist form of Marxism that strongly attracts many people in countries on the verge of rapid industrialization. One key element, as Adam Ulam has convincingly argued, has been Marxism's combination of an eventual promise of "anarchism pure and simple . . . the most violent protest against industrialism" with the insistence that industrialization is inevitable. To those in underdeveloped countries who have, for various reasons, yearned for industrial development, Marxism has been an ideology that undermines the arguments of traditional elites about the possibility of avoiding industrialization, while it provides reassurances that the suffering produced by industrialization will eventually be justified by the creation of paradise on Earth.[2]

Another attraction of Marxism-Leninism may well be precisely its authoritarianism. In *Escape from Freedom* Erich Fromm contended that the successful emergence of an authoritarian Calvinist religion in the sixteenth century and of the Nazi Party in Germany in the 1930s had been possible because of the widespread longing for certainty and a sense of belonging among people whose world and world view had been shattered by social changes.[3] If this line of analysis is reasonably accurate, the onset of industrialization in the twentieth century should

1. W.W. Rostow, *The Stages of Economic Growth: A Non-Communist Manifesto* (London: Cambridge University Press, 1960), pp. 162–64.

2. Adam Ulam, "The Historical Role of Marxism and the Soviet System," *World Politics*, vol. 8 (October 1955), pp. 28–29.

3. Erich Fromm, *Escape from Freedom* (Rinehart, 1941), chaps. 3 and 6.

often have similar consequences in Russia. In the early part of the century, the end of serfdom, the national disgrace in three wars (the Crimean War, the Russo-Japanese War, and World War I), the beginning of rapid industrialization, and the collapse of an absolute monarchy closely tied to an official state religion should have produced, if Fromm is correct, a strong propensity to "escape from freedom."

Lenin certainly seemed to have sensed such an attitude in the Russian people of the time. Although he spoke of "all power to the soviets" in terms that appeared to promise democracy, he was scornful of the "parliamentarism" of the West. A little over a month before the revolution, he wrote of the governmental "vacillation that torments the people," and he predicted that the end of such vacillation after the revolution would solidify the popular support for the party.[4] And, in fact, many of the features of the Bolshevism that he—and, even more, Stalin—espoused had many parallels with the Calvinism that Fromm has described: the rigid determinism; the distinction between the elect and the damned; the possibility of membership in an exclusive party of comrades (the community of saints); and, though no God, a godlike dictator.

But what happens when the situation changes? What happens when industrialization progresses to the point where it becomes irreversible and no longer needs ideological defense, where people begin clamoring for a better life today instead of waiting for a future utopia? What happens when the psychology of the people themselves begins to change?

The Population in Flux

For some, questions about the consequences of change in the Soviet people have little relevance to an analysis of the Soviet future. They flatly deny that any change has been taking place. For example, Hedrick Smith in his very successful book, *The Russians*, emphasizes the influence of the Russian past on the present and the future and argues that after the social upheavals in the 1920s and 1930s, "perhaps Russia has seemed gradually to be returning to many of its old ways." He ends the book with his wife's comment, "It was the same under the czars. They're the same people."[5]

4. V.I. Lenin, "Marksizm i vosstanie," in V.I. Lenin, *Polnoe sobranie sochinenii* (Moscow: Gospolitizdat, 1962), vol. 24, p. 247.
5. Hedrick Smith, *The Russians* (Quadrangle, 1976), pp. 505, 509.

The level of sales of *The Russians* suggests that we want to be reassured that all our old stereotypes are valid and will continue to be so. But we should not be misled. The statistical handbooks do not point to a static population: the population of the Soviet Union in the 1920s had much the same statistical profile as that of Mexico or Egypt in the 1970s, but it has changed enormously over the last fifty years—and is still changing, for the USSR remains a partially underdeveloped country by Western standards.

First, of course, the Soviet Union has become more urbanized. Most people in prerevolutionary Russia lived in villages of several hundred inhabitants and worked their strips of land on the outskirts. Few lived in large towns. In 1926 only 12 percent of the population lived in cities with over 20,000 people and only 7 percent in cities with over 100,000.[6]

In comparison with the United States, the Soviet Union is still in mid-urbanization. The mass movement of people from the farm to the city, which has virtually been completed in the United States, still goes on in the Soviet Union and will continue into the twenty-first century. It has, however, already affected the way in which tens of millions of Soviet citizens live. The percentage of people living in towns of at least 20,000 rose to 36 percent by 1959 and 48 percent by 1975.[7] The increase in the number of people living in cities of at least 100,000 population was just as dramatic:[8]

Year	Number of people	Percentage of total population
1926	9,990,000	7
1939	30,370,000	18
1956	43,000,000	22
1965	65,980,000	29
1979	98,850,000	38

6. Calculated from *Itogi vsesoiuznoi perepisi naseleniia 1959 goda, SSSR (svodnyi tom)* (Moscow: Gosstatizdat, 1962), pp. 13, 35.

7. *Narodnoe khoziaistvo SSSR v 1974 g., Statisticheskii ezhegodnik* (Moscow: Statistika, 1975), p. 32.

8. Frank Lorimer, *The Population of the Soviet Union: History and Prospects* (Geneva: The League of Nations, 1946), pp. 112, 250–53; *Narodnoe khoziaistvo SSSR v 1956 godu, Statisticheskii ezhegodnik* (Moscow: Gosstatizdat, 1957), pp. 30–31; *Narodnoe khoziaistvo SSSR v 1964 g., Statisticheskii ezhegodnik* (Moscow: Statistika, 1964), pp. 22–31; Tsentral'noe statisticheskoe upravlenie SSSR, *Naselenie SSSR, Po dannym Vsesoiuznoi perepisi naseleniia 1979 goda* (Moscow: Politizdat, 1980), pp. 3, 11–15.

Table 2-1. *Educational Distribution of the Soviet Population Ten Years of Age and Over, 1939–79*

Millions

	Education			
Year	Complete higher	Complete secondary	Incomplete secondary[a]	No secondary[b]
1939	1.2	14.7[c]		131.3
1959	3.8	19.5	35.4	103.9
1970	8.3	39.4	47.3	101.7
1979	14.8	71.8	52.5	78.9

Sources: *Narodnoe khoziaistvo SSSR v 1975 g., Statisticheskii ezhegodnik* (Moscow: Statistika, 1976), p. 36; Tsentral'noe statisticheskoe upravlenie SSSR, *Naselenie SSSR, Po dannym Vsesoiuznoi perepisi naseleniia 1979 goda* (Moscow: Politizdat, 1980), p. 19.

a. At least seven years of education for 1939 and 1959; at least eight years for 1970 and 1979. Before 1961 secondary school began with the eighth grade; after 1961 it began with the ninth. Anyone who completed the seventh grade before 1961 or the eighth grade afterward is counted as having incomplete secondary education in the Soviet statistics.

b. Less than seven years of education for 1939 and 1959; less than eight years for 1970 and 1979.

c. The figures for 1939 are not divided between incomplete and complete secondary education.

Table 2-2. *Number of People in Occupations of Different Status Levels, 1939, 1959, and 1970*

Millions

Type of occupation	1939	1959	1970
White collar	11.580	18.765	30.820
Skilled labor	9.595	21.230	33.485
Medium-skilled labor	6.550	11.680	11.975
Least-skilled labor	9.935	10.450	8.075
Higher-skilled labor in agriculture	2.690	3.500	3.925
Unskilled labor in agriculture	32.075	30.365	18.680

Source: Jerry F. Hough and Merle Fainsod, *How the Soviet Union Is Governed* (Harvard University Press, 1979), pp. 564–65. The precise definitions of the categories and the way in which the figures were calculated are described in the original.

Between 1965 (the year after Brezhnev came into power) and 1979, the number of people living in cities that were already at the 100,000 level in 1965 increased by 18,679,000, double the total number who lived in such cities in 1926.

Second, the level of education among the Soviet people has risen sharply. Unfortunately, the 1926 census did not include a question about the citizen's years of education, limiting itself to an inquiry about literacy. It placed the literacy rate at 57 percent for those between the ages of nine and forty-nine, but many of the "literates" had little, if any, exposure to formal schooling. Even among members of the Communist party in 1927, 27 percent had had less than four years of school.[9] By 1939 the census had begun exploring the educational level of the population more thoroughly; it found that after a decade of intense educational effort by the regime, much of it directed toward adults, only 11 percent of the population aged ten or older had finished as much as seven years of schooling. By 1959 this figure had risen to 36 percent, by 1970 to 48 percent, and by 1979 to 64 percent. It stood at 86 percent for those who lived in the city and were employed.[10] As table 2-1 indicates, the core of people with a high-school diploma or better had become quite substantial by the late 1970s.

Third, the occupational structure in the Soviet Union has been undergoing transformation. The large-scale migration of people from the country to the city is of course accompanied by a shift from rural to urban occupations. Industrialization requires a continuous expansion in the number of white-collar and skilled blue-collar jobs in the city. In the early stages of industrialization, the number of unskilled urban jobs increases as well, though eventually mechanization begins to reduce that number.

The scale of the change in the occupational distribution is clearly indicated in table 2-2, and it hardly needs mentioning that the distribution before the great industrialization drive of 1928–29 was skewed even more strongly in the direction of unskilled agricultural and laboring jobs than it was in 1939. With respect to values, the most important change that has been occurring is not in the skill level of the jobs held, but in their status. The Russian peasants were not the independent farmers of American lore, but "the dark people," as the educated called them. Movement upward on the list of the job categories shown in table 2-2 meant not only upward mobility in a real sense, but surely in most cases a higher self-esteem.

9. For the literacy figure, *Itogi vsesoiuznoi perepisi naseleniia 1970 goda* (Moscow: Statistika, 1972), vol. 3, p. 570; for the statistic on the education of party members, *Partiinaia zhizn'*, no. 21 (November 1977), p. 29.

10. Tsentral'noe statisticheskoe upravlenie SSSR, *Naselenie SSSR, Po dannym Vsesoiuznoi perepisi naseleniia 1979 goda* (Moscow: Politizdat, 1980), pp. 20, 21.

Table 2-3. *Percentage of Soviet Citizens with a Complete Secondary Education, by Age Group, 1959 and 1970*

Age group	1959	1970
20–29	22.6	52.6
30–39	20.6	33.3
40–49	13.1	24.0
50–59	9.2	15.7
60 and over	4.9	8.1
Total, 20 and over	15.8	28.0

Sources: Calculated from *Itogi vsesoiuznoi perepisi naseleniia 1959 goda*, *CCCP (svodny tom)* (Moscow: Gosstatizdat, 1962), pp. 74–75, and *Itogi vsesoiuznoi perepisi naseleniia 1970 goda* (Moscow: Statistika, 1972), vol. 3, pp. 6–7.

Although discussions of social change usually focus—as this section has—upon statistics for society as a whole, one point deserves special emphasis. Social change does not usually affect all elements of the population in the same way, and, above all, it does not affect all age groups to the same extent. Flight from the country to the city is predominantly a flight of the young; a rise in the educational level of a society is achieved largely through greater education for the young and a gradual dying out of the less-educated elderly; a change in the occupational structure tends to mean the movement of the better-educated young into the new jobs that require the skills they possess or can acquire. As a result, rapid social change is likely to maximize many of the differences between the young and the old.

This has happened in the Soviet Union during recent decades. The best available statistics on the generational differences produced by social change deal with the level of education. But even a statistic showing a rise in the percentage of the population with a secondary school diploma from 16 percent in 1959 to 28 percent in 1970 (as seen in table 2-3) still does not indicate how drastic a change has been taking place among the relatively young. The gradual aging of the young, along with the acquisition of more education by some of them in later life, will eventually spread the new educational achievements throughout the population, but in the period of transition—which stretches over decades—the differences between the old and the young can be dramatic indeed.

The Party Members and the Attentive Public

In any country only a small part of the population pays much attention to the political sphere, except to isolated issues or events. In Italy, one poll in the 1960s discovered that 40 percent of the respondents could not name a single political leader in the country and that 62 percent said that they "never follow the accounts of political and governmental affairs."[11] In the United States, public awareness of the names of a few leaders is much higher, but political scientists consider only 15 to 20 percent of the population to be part of the truly "attentive public." Suffice it to say that in June 1979 just 30 percent of the American public knew that the United States and the Soviet Union were the countries engaged in the second strategic arms limitation talks (SALT II), and only 51 percent knew that the United States needed to import petroleum.[12]

In analyzing the Soviet Union, too, one needs to think of the population in differentiated terms. Because of that country's level of development, one would expect the degree of political apathy and noninvolvement there to be closer to that in Italy than to that in the United States, and, in fact, the impressionistic evidence suggests that this is so. Although few can have avoided learning the name of Brezhnev, the great majority of the Soviet people are little interested in politics and the policy process, at least in other than having grievances about this or that policy and perhaps speaking out on some question at the place of work or in the local neighborhood.

But, in comparative terms, the question is not whether 80 or 90 percent of the people are essentially uninformed and noninvolved, but whether there is a 10 or 20 percent core who constitute an attentive public and another 20 to 30 percent who have a sporadic interest in what is going on.

The answer to this question depends in large part upon one's definition of *politics*. Americans usually use the word in a personalized sense. That is, politics has to do with the fortunes of George Bush, with the strategy of President Carter in his struggle with Senator Ken-

11. Gabriel A. Almond and Sidney Verba, *The Civic Culture: Political Attitudes and Democracy in Five Nations* (Princeton University Press, 1963), pp. 89, 96.
12. *New York Times*, June 12, 1979, and June 13, 1979.

nedy, or perhaps the conflict between the former secretary of state
Cyrus Vance, and the national security adviser, Zbigniew Brzezinski.
By that definition, there may be a relatively wide potential attentive
public in the Soviet Union (where there is a great interest in rumors of
any type, but especially personal ones), but on such political questions
there is little to which the citizen can be attentive. Information about
the views, let alone the political maneuverings, of individual leaders is
tightly controlled. Even a person who is among the 5,000 to 10,000
best-informed citizens in the country may have a sense of who is up
and who is down in the political leadership, but may be unable to find
any clue to the reasons why.

Politics can, however, have another meaning. It can refer to the
policy problems facing a country or a local community and the range of
possible governmental actions to try to cope with them. Political
awareness and involvement can mean having information and opinions
on these problems, and political activity can mean taking steps to influence the decisions about them—steps that can include conversations
to persuade friends, participation on committees, or the writing of
books and articles. Since Soviet newspapers, journals, and books publish debates on these kinds of political issues, the attentive public that
follows them is much larger than that which can follow high politics in
a personalistic sense.

The actual size of the Soviet attentive public on policy issues is difficult to judge, and it no doubt varies with the issue and the background
of the citizen. One Soviet poll on citizen interest in commentary on international life found that 28 percent of the collective farmers in the
sample claimed such an interest, 29 percent of the workers, 39 percent
of the students, 40 percent of the engineering-technical personnel, and
55 percent of the party and soviet employees.[13] Although these are
only claims and surely exaggerated ones, they may still suggest the
range of sporadic interest in broader political questions within the population.

Information on the number of Soviet citizens who follow policy
questions fairly consistently is lacking, but conceivably it too is comparatively large. We speak of the rule of the Communist party in the
Soviet Union and are aware that admission to the party is not open to

13. V.I. Brovikov and I.V. Popovich, *Sovremennye problemy politicheskoi infor-
matsii i agitatsii* (Moscow: Mysl', 1969), p. 29.

everyone but is treated as a privilege by the regime. That only 6 percent of the population are party members is a statistic frequently cited.
We know that many join the party for reasons of career advancement
rather than ideological fervor, but we still tend to exclude party members—including, or perhaps especially, the more opportunistic ones—
from our usual generalizations about the politically apathetic Russian
public. And yet, as mentioned earlier, some 21 percent of all Soviet
men between the ages of thirty-one and sixty are party members—and
more than 50 percent of the male college graduates in that age group. If
the Soviet attentive public is even roughly on this scale, it is not much
different from that in Western countries.

How can it be that over half of the male college graduates over thirty
are members of the party when it seems so exclusive to us—and when
party membership totals 17 million in a country of nearly 270 million
people? The explanation is that two groups are recruited into the party
in very limited numbers: youth and women. Although the official minimum age for party admission is eighteen, few are admitted before their
mid-twenties. (In 1966 the average age of admission was thirty-one,
and in 1975 it was twenty-seven.) Therefore, the proportion of those
over thirty who are party members is 11 percent rather than 6 percent,
and if those over sixty are excluded, it is 12.5 percent. Also, because
only some 7 percent of women between the ages of thirty-one and sixty—4 percent of all adult women—become party members, the proportion for men of this age group rises considerably.[14]

What has occurred is a tremendous change in the nature of party
membership since the early days of the Soviet regime. After Lenin's
death in 1924, the regime for a while recruited new members almost
exclusively from the worker and peasant classes, and by 1932, 92 percent of all Communists had been employed as workers or peasants
when they joined the party. By contrast, in 1928 only 1.2 percent of
employed persons with higher and specialized secondary education
were members of the party. Stalin's policy at that time was to enroll
workers and peasants in their late teens and early twenties and then to
create a new political and administrative elite by encouraging the new

14. The material on party membership is drawn from Jerry F. Hough, *The Soviet
Union and Social Science Theory* (Harvard University Press, 1977), pp. 125–39; and Jer-
ry F. Hough and Merle Fainsod, *How the Soviet Union Is Governed* (Harvard University
Press, 1979), pp. 320–61.

party members to move into white-collar jobs or even to return to college as adults if they were capable of doing so.

Once he had created his new elite, however, Stalin changed the policy of party admission (in the late 1930s but with an interlude during World War II), and this new policy has remained in force until the present day. Since the society had become settled, the party leaders had little reason to choose among prospective members on the basis of professions of loyalty or ideological zeal by twenty-one-year-olds. They decided to wait until candidates for party membership were old enough to have demonstrated their dedication to the party in deeds as well as words—a dedication that was largely judged by performance on the job.

Quite a few workers and peasants were still admitted into the party, especially after Stalin's death. In 1970, for example, some 28 percent of the members were workers by current occupation and 10 percent were collective farmers. Many of these did experience some rise into administrative posts later in life, but the bulk of the administrative elite—and certainly most of those destined for its upper levels—joined the party after finishing college rather than before. The figure of 50 percent membership for male college graduates over thirty correctly indicates that it has become virtually automatic for a man with the propensity and ability to rise in his career to become a party member, so long as he keeps away from open political dissidence and religious observances.

The changes that occurred in the party's admission policy after World War II have important implications that we have still not absorbed into our understanding of the Soviet system.

First, the old Western notions of a conflict between "red" and "expert," which had a basis in reality in the 1920s, have become irrelevant today. Although many of the cultural and scientific intelligentsia avoid party membership (primarily because they do not want the committee work and political assignments that come with it), the kind of expertise thought appropriate for administrative or supervisory work is normally a prerequisite for party membership instead of being in conflict with it.

Second, the requirement of party membership for almost all significant administrative jobs does not mean that the administrative system is staffed by the most opportunistic. The fact that party membership is expected of people with the potential to rise means, paradoxically, that party membership tends to become irrelevant to promotion. Since all likely candidates are party members, the selection must be made on other criteria.

Third, "party control" at the lowest administrative levels often has a very different meaning from the one we are apt to assume. The Communist party does have a centralized hierarchy of territorial committees and full-time officials, and one of its primary functions is to ensure that central decisions are carried out. This hierarchy does exercise supervision over the other institutions of the system—the governmental agencies, the economic enterprises, the trade unions, and so forth—and this supervision extends to the creation of primary party organizations in every place of work where there are three Communists.

Yet when Soviet sources mention that a high proportion of the trade union activists at a factory are party members, we should not automatically see the hand of Moscow intruding there, with these party members as its agents. It is simply inevitable that any adult institution must have a large proportion of Communists among its active members, for those who are active will usually join the party (except, perhaps, women).

Similarly, when the primary party organization or its executive committee discusses the work of the enterprise and its manager, it occasionally may act in response to a higher decision, but more often it functions like a departmental meeting in an American university. The Communists who take on voluntary trade union work or attend meetings of party committees are doing so for the same reasons that people engage in committee work in the West—because they have to, because they want to make contacts, because they want to further their careers by impressing higher officials with their energy and quality of judgment, and maybe sometimes because they want to influence a decision or have an effect on local conditions of importance to them.

Finally, so far as there is an overlap between the party membership and the attentive public, the statistics about party members may give some clue about what is going on within the attentive public. Undoubtedly, some of the worker and peasant members are essentially apolitical, and many of the cultural intellectuals, the natural scien-

Table 2-4. *Distribution of Party Members, by Level of Education,
1927–77*[a]

Thousands; numbers in parentheses are percentages

	Education					
Years	Less than four years	Four to seven or eight years[a]	Incomplete secondary[a]	Complete secondary	Incomplete higher	Complete higher
1927	310 (27)	720[b] (63)			105[b] (9)	9.6 (1)
1937	483 (24)	887 (45)	228 (12)	228 (12)	49 (2)	108 (5)
1947	510 (8)	2,100 (35)	1,527 (25)	1,325 (22)	136 (2)	453 (8)
1957	353 (5)	2,102 (28)	2,207 (29)	1,696 (23)	267 (4)	870 (12)
1967	. . .	2,851 (22)	3,417 (27)	3,993 (32)	326 (3)	2,097 (16)
1977	. . .	2,182 (14)	3,154 (20)	6,268 (39)	380 (2)	4,009 (25)

Source: *Partiinaia zhizn'*, no. 21 (November 1977), p. 29. Figures are rounded.
a. See note a in table 2–1.
b. The figures for 1927 do not distinguish between four-to-seven years of elementary education and incomplete secondary education, or between complete secondary and incomplete higher education.

Table 2-5. *Party Representation among Men and Women over Thirty,
by Level of Education, 1970*

Level of education	Percent in party	Percent of males in party	Percent of females in party
Doctor of science[a]	55.0	. . .	. . .
Candidate of science[a]	49.1	. . .	. . .
Complete higher	35.5	52	15
Incomplete higher	30.2	43	13
Complete secondary	23.6	39	10
Incomplete secondary[b]	13.3	22	6
Complete and incomplete elementary	3.8	8	1
Total	10.6	20	4

Source: Hough and Fainsod, *How the Soviet Union Is Governed*, p. 346. The figure for total number in the party, by education, could be calculated fairly precisely for 1970, a census year. The distribution by sex required more extrapolation. The figure for each sex should, however, be accurate within five percentage points for those with complete and incomplete higher education and within several percentage points for the others given.
a. The figures for doctors and candidates of science are for 1971 instead of 1970, and no attempt is made to exclude those thirty years of age or younger. But 1971 should be little different from 1970, and neither group should include many people under thirty. The extrapolations for males and females in this group are too uncertain for inclusion.
b. See note a in table 2-1.

tists, the women,[15] and those under thirty who are not party members take a keen interest in public issues. Nevertheless, tables 2-4 and 2-5 indicate not only that the party is not an egalitarian body in its recruitment policy—the usual conclusion drawn in the West—but that the core of the reasonably politically active in Soviet society is both increasing rapidly in size and changing in the quality of its educational preparation.

Changing Political Values

One can cite a great deal of sociological data on the educational and occupational distribution of a population, but the question remains, what does it all mean? Does a rising educational level mean a people more assertive toward the political authorities and less tolerant of authoritarian measures—and maybe even of an authoritarian regime? Or are the educational and occupational statistics merely another sign that the Soviet elite is becoming a settled establishment, very conservative in the face of any possible change that might threaten its position and well-being, whether it be totalitarian changes or democratization?

When this kind of question is discussed in reference to the West or the third world, the analysis tends to run in a single direction. As Karl Deutsch has noted, "A good deal of research shows that in general people with little education prefer to be told only one side of a problem. When presented with two conflicting views, they tend to become confused and angry . . . better educated people tend in most countries to feel angry and insulted when presented only one side of an issue. They want to hear all sides and make their own decisions."[16] In the political sphere, too, public opinion polls consistently show a strong cor-

15. In school, girls provide much the greater proportion of the active members of the various types of student government activity, and even in young adulthood they remain quite active in comparison with men. Soviet studies show that their participation drops sharply after marriage and especially after the birth of children. Whether their interest declines at the same rate is more problematical. The rules of party membership require that a prospective member not only agree with the party program but actively participate in party work. It is this latter requirement, not a lack of interest, that may keep many women out of the party; it is extremely difficult for a woman to combine a full-time job *and* an active political life, with the kind of housekeeping and child-raising responsibilities imposed on her by a society that is male chauvinistic in this respect.

16. Karl W. Deutsch, *Politics and Government: How People Decide Their Fate* (Houghton Mifflin, 1970), p. 305.

relation between level of education and support for issues that involve individual freedom and tolerance of diversity.

In a constitutional democracy, of course, support of civil liberties is hardly inconsistent with conservatism about the fundamentals of the political system. Indeed, one might argue that the polls simply demonstrate that the Western educational systems have been indoctrinating the population with the norms of the political system and that the more time citizens spend in the educational institutions, the more thoroughly indoctrinated they are likely to be.

Nevertheless, Western scholars have argued that a similar link exists between education and democratic values in third world countries where the schools attempt to build support for nondemocratic systems. The existence of a middle class and the existence of a certain level of education among the population are said to be preconditions for Western-style democracy, and the development of such phenomena is widely thought to undercut the support for authoritarian regimes. Although the timing of the fall of the Iranian shah was a surprise to most, no one thought that the shah's authority as an absolute monarch would survive many years of his modernization program.

Scholars, it should be added, have also seen a link between education and the development of nationalism among large ethnic minorities within a country. This is especially true of groups who retain their own language and who are sufficiently concentrated to entertain thoughts of forming an independent nation. When such an ethnic group consists overwhelmingly of uneducated peasants, it usually does not have enough leaders to carry out a revolution, or even many members interested in one. Very few have the training to benefit personally from an expulsion of members of the dominant nationality from administrative and professional jobs in the area.

But an increase in the proportion of the urbanized and the better-educated among an ethnic minority group changes the situation radically. If the central language (for example, English in Quebec) were to be replaced by the language of the local group (in this instance, French) as the language of work, this would remove an important barrier to the promotion of members of the minority into top professional and managerial jobs. In fact, if the language of work could be changed rapidly and by force of law, numerous vacancies for such promotion would be created, for the old incumbents would often be compelled to leave. The increase in the strength of the separatist movement in Quebec, after its long-term impotence, corresponds closely to the rise in the number of people with the education to gain personally from an independent or autonomous Quebec.

If the experience of other countries is any guide, the Soviet Union faces not one Quebec problem, but perhaps twenty. Those of Russian nationality have never constituted much more than half the Soviet population since the incorporation of the Western Ukraine, Western Belorussia, and the Baltic States in 1939 and 1940. And this proportion then slipped from 55 percent in 1959 to 52 percent in 1979 because of the higher birthrates among many of the non-Russian groups. The non-Russian nationalities each speak a separate language, and, except for the Jews, the Germans, and the Poles, the major ones have an identifiable territorial base. Indeed, the regime has given each of these non-dispersed nationalities its own union republic or autonomous republic, where the local language as well as Russian is official and where the development of the local culture is encouraged. In addition, as part of its industrialization drive, the regime has pushed the acquisition of education among all the Soviet peoples and, as was seen above, has had the kind of success that paradoxically has created political difficulties in other multinational societies.

The question, of course, is whether these generalizations about Western social science are relevant to the development of political attitudes in the Soviet Union. In particular, are the changing educational and occupational patterns found among Soviet citizens of different ages reflected in generational differences in political attitudes?

The question is difficult to answer. The Soviet Union publishes few polls on politically sensitive subjects, and in the polls that do exist it is not always easy to distinguish between a mere age difference and a generational one. For example, polls show young people going to movies and plays much more frequently than older ones, but if the pattern is similar to that in other countries, the young will go less frequently as they age. On the other hand, differences in attitudes about the need for parental consent for marriage are more likely to be enduring generational ones.[17] In other cases it is difficult to tell.

Nevertheless, there are indications that politically important vari-

17. Iu. Arutiunian and Iu. Kakhk, eds., *Sotsiologisticheskie ocherki o Sovetskoi Estonii* (Tallin: Periodika, 1979), pp. 52, 115, 119.

ations of a generational kind do exist. Soviet sources use the word "generation" (*pokolenie*) easily and frequently. They may express pride that the younger generation has not had to make the sacrifices of the older ones, as well as concern that it (especially its youngest members) may not have the dedication or the discipline of the older generations. To some extent, this attitude is simply an expression of the age-old concern about the decline in values among the young, but sometimes it comes out with very different moral overtones and in these instances at least rests on a very different base.

Consider, for example, an article on "the succession of generations" (*preemstvennost' pokolenii*) written in 1965 by the assistant to the minister of defense for supervision of military-educational institutions, Marshal P.A. Rotmistrov.[18] Marshal Rotmistrov, then a man of sixty-four who referred to his contemporaries as "we . . . of the older generation," wrote glowingly of the new soldier: "If we now received draftees into the army and the navy with the kind of preparation which our youth had in the 1940s, then it would be very difficult for us to teach them to master modern weapons." What is especially significant is that Rotmistrov assumed that a change in values came with the higher level of preparation. Throughout the article he pointed out that this new man had to be led by very different methods from those used in the past, emphasizing "how important it is to respect subordinates in communications with them."

Unfortunately, we still observe cases when old methods of teaching and training are used in the new, changed conditions and when the fact that the soldier of our Motherland is, first of all, a literate man is given insufficient attention. . . . Rudeness and an offensive tone in relation to a subordinate is particularly intolerable. But let's suppose that the senior happens to act tactlessly towards a junior or unjustifiably offends a subordinate. What should be done then? He is obligated to find the courage in himself to apologize.[19]

A decade later an article on military discipline made the same point about the growth in literacy among the soldiers and warned that "they are more demanding about the argumentation and cultural level of the efforts to influence them."[20] In 1978 Brezhnev demanded a change in the Soviet mass media, especially in their coverage of foreign events, for the same reason:

18. *Krasnaia zvezda* [Red Star], November 25, 1965.
19. Ibid., p. 2.
20. Ibid., December 18, 1975, p. 3.

Soviet man now, as never before, is politically literate and active. He justly makes high demands on the media of mass communication. . . . It is time to ensure that information on international affairs be more accessible and factual, that international commentary follow closely on the fresh trail of events, and that generalizations be not the repetition of well-worn bromides but deep and well-argued analysis of the facts of international life. That is what is necessary.

Brezhnev's audience—a plenary session of the Party Central Committee—responded with applause.[21]

This is not of course to say that the Soviet citizens, let alone the better-educated ones, are poised to march into the streets to overthrow the Communist regime. As Crane Brinton accurately said long ago, one of the crucial signs that a system is about to collapse is usually some widespread awareness that it is, in fact, in trouble.[22] In this respect, all observers of the Soviet scene agree that the public mood is very different from what it is in Poland.

The Soviet government has thus far been skillful in the way it has tied the fate of many individuals in the country to the fate of the regime. By admitting such a broad range of the educated public into the party, it has provided full opportunities for upward social mobility for those who avoid dissidence, while giving everyone in the managerial class reason to wonder what the impact of an anti-Communist revolution would be upon him or her personally. No post-Soviet regime would be able to function without using former Communists at all levels in the civil service. But since there would surely be commissions to sort out who had been "good" Communists and who had been "bad," few can look forward to such a change.

These considerations, it should be noted, are as relevant for the non-Russians as for the Russians. Separatist movements have been the strongest in areas where the minority's upward mobility has been blocked by the dominant group's tendency to monopolize the best jobs, but the party leadership in the Soviet Union has been keenly sensitive to this danger. Besides using the stick of repression against politically active nationalists, the leadership has enrolled members of the different nationalities in the party in rough proportion to the educational level among them, although with lesser success among the nationalities seized in 1939–40 (see table 2-6). It has also conducted a vigorous affirmative action program to give members of the local nationality politi-

21. *Pravda*, November 28, 1975, p. 2.
22. Crane Brinton, *The Anatomy of Revolution* (Norton, 1938), pp. 80–81.

Table 2-6. *Level of Party Membership and Education among Nationalities, 1970*

Nationality	Percentage of people with at least a secondary education[a] (1)	Percentage of party members[b] (2)	"Predicted" percentage of party members[c] (3)	Over-representation or under-representation in party[d] (4)
Georgians	41	11.6	13.4	-1.8
Armenians	31	11.3	10.4	0.9
Russians	26	10.3	9.0	1.3
Ukrainians	24	8.0	8.4	-0.4
Estonians	24	5.9	8.4	-2.5
Latvians	24	5.5	8.4	-2.9
Azerbaidzhani	23	10.3	8.1	2.2
Belorussians	21	8.2	7.6	0.6
Uzbeks	20	6.9	7.3	-0.4
Kazakhs	19	10.0	7.0	3.0
Kirghizians	19	7.3	7.0	0.3
Turkmens	17	6.6	6.4	0.2
Tadzhiks	17	6.2	6.4	-0.2
Lithuanians	16	5.1	6.1	-1.0
Moldavians	11	3.5	4.7	-1.2

Source: Hough and Fainsod, *How the Soviet Union Is Governed*, pp. 352–53.

a. Among those ten years of age and over.

b. Among those twenty years of age and over.

c. "Predicted" from a regression analysis used to determine the "typical" relationship between the proportion of a nationality with complete secondary education and the proportion of that nationality in the party.

d. In percentage points. Calculated by subtracting column 3 from column 2.

cal and administrative jobs in the local area, even in preference to better-qualified Russians.

The Soviet regime has also been successful in identifying itself with the achievement of Russian national goals—and Soviet national goals to the extent that non-Russians perceive them. From the time when Stalin emphasized the building of "socialism in one country" to today, when there are still continual references to the victory in World War II (the Great Patriotic War) in the media, the leadership has played hard upon the national theme. And over this period, the Soviet Union has gone from a backward European power to one of the two great superpowers. The close relationship between communism and the achievement of national goals in the Soviet Union must be a prime reason why the Soviet regime has been so much more stable than many others in Eastern Europe, where the relationship is reversed.

For a Russian, thoughts of democratization must at best produce feelings of ambivalence. The establishment of a constitutional democracy in the Soviet Union would surely be accompanied by the collapse of the Communist regimes of Eastern Europe, and many of the politicians in that area would no doubt find it profitable to appeal to the resentments that have built up under Russian domination. In the USSR itself, nationalist parties would most likely arise within the republics, and many of these might well choose independence. Therefore, democratization would undoubtedly result in a great reduction in the national power of Russia, and would bring sharply to the fore the question of whether and how Russia would use military force "to preserve the union." Thus the nagging doubts of members of the Russian educated public about the consequences of democratization for themselves personally are reinforced by considerations of patriotic feelings.

Nevertheless, a change in political values need not lead to revolution to be politically relevant. An intelligent leadership—especially one that does not have competitive elections in which to offer up individual leaders as scapegoats for political problems—should try to rule in a way to minimize the conflicts with its people. If the people change their ideas about what is appropriate, an intelligent leadership should try as much as possible to adjust its methods of rule to accommodate them.

If one thinks back to the features of the Stalin system that corresponded most closely to Erich Fromm's analysis in *Escape from Freedom*—deterministic laws of history, a dogmatic and simplistic world view, a narrow party of the elect, and a God-like dictator—one is struck by how much they have since changed. Perhaps these changes have nothing to do with the shifts in the population that have been the subject of this chapter, but it is hard to avoid the feeling that the two are related. Marshal Rotmistrov's arguments for a different relationship between the officer and the new literate soldier were obviously just as relevant to the relationship between the civilian leadership and the civilian population—and Rotmistrov must have been aware of this fact. Indeed, he may well have been articulating in the military sphere a philosophy that Brezhnev and other civilian leaders were expressing in private, to defend the more relaxed regime they were instituting.

One could go further. Crane Brinton argued that the stability of a regime depends not only on the depth of resentment on the part of the discontented but also on the self-confidence that those who benefit from a system have in defending it.[23] A loss of a sense of legitimacy among the elite is often more crucial than among the masses. There is no evidence that the political and managerial elite have lost the self-confidence needed, for example, to face an open challenge in the streets, but their feeling about the legitimacy of present levels of re-pression may be another matter. It is, after all, the broad elite—the at-tentive public—who suffer the most in a direct sense from the restric-tions on culture, publications, travel abroad, and so forth, and the pressure to move toward the looser kinds of control found in Hungary or Poland, or perhaps in most right-wing authoritarian regimes, may be strong within the Communist party itself.

From this perspective, the most important statistic in this chapter may not be the high proportion of the young with secondary education, but rather the sharp rise in the educational level that is beginning to oc-cur among the middle-aged. It was in the 1950s that a large number of teenagers first began getting a secondary education (see table 2-3); therefore, the vanguard is now in its early forties. Since this is also the group that reached the age of political awareness at the time Khru-shchev was denouncing Stalin, its overall political complexion might differ significantly from that of its predecessors.

The men who must make the decisions on how to respond to a chang-ing and growing attentive public are, however, of a very different gen-eration. Most of the members of the present Politburo went to secon-dary school not in the 1950s, but in the 1920s—or in some cases earlier. Even if the next general secretary is much younger than expected, he will probably still have been at least eighteen at the outbreak of World War II. It is men now in their fifties, sixties, and seventies who must be given the most attention in this book. But it is how they respond to a society vastly different from the one in which they grew up that will determine their success—and perhaps even their ability to survive—as rulers.

23. Ibid., pp. 64–71.

3

The Four Generations:
The Formative Experiences

DEVELOPING countries are prone to drastic change in their political systems. A coup d'état may not only remove a leader but also transform the way in which a country is governed. An entire ruling elite may be driven into exile and replaced by men with radically different views. In the process the societies often pass through a series of convulsions. Russia has been a developing country for most of the last 100 years, and in the best of circumstances it would have gone through difficult periods. As it turned out, few countries have suffered such a series of devastating blows to their population and the fabric of their society as Russia experienced in the first half of the twentieth century.

Already in the second half of the nineteenth century, Russia began having a familiar problem. The development of better medical care, partly because of reforms instituted by the tsar, lowered the mortality rate while the birthrate remained high. So far as can be estimated, the natural annual increase in the population rose from 9 persons per 1,000 to 13 persons per 1,000.[1] Russian agriculture had difficulty keeping up, and in the wake of agricultural problems and then defeat in war with Japan, Russia was racked by a year and a half of revolution in 1905–06. Less than a decade later, it entered World War I, during which about 2 million deaths occurred in the army alone.[2] Dissatisfaction with the tsar's management of the war contributed directly to his overthrow in February 1917, but the revolutionary upsurge continued and Lenin's Bolsheviks rode it to power in October of that year.

The October Revolution itself was relatively easy, relatively bloodless for an event of its magnitude, but it was followed by more than three years of civil war of a very different nature. "Red" and "White" armies moved back and forth across Russia, with both sides often

1. Frank Lorimer, *The Population of the Soviet Union: History and Prospects* (Geneva: The League of Nations, 1946), p. 11.
2. Ibid., p. 40.

showing the savagery that is customary in civil wars. The virtual collapse of the economy meant increased cold and hunger and a greatly lowered resistance to disease. Typhus alone killed over 2 million people in the four years 1919–23, and typhoid, dysentery, and cholera claimed another million in this period. In all, the best estimate of the number of excess deaths from 1914 to 1926—that is, deaths above the number that would normally have been expected—is 16 million. Another 2 million people emigrated, and 10 million fewer children were born than would have been in normal times.[3]

Most of the 1920s was a period of respite and reconstruction, but then in 1928 another assault on the population began. Frightened by growing difficulties in grain procurements and determined to start a rapid industrialization program, Stalin forced through collectivization of the Soviet countryside. The peasants resisted, guerrilla war broke out, and more than 1 million peasants were exiled to camps in the north and in Siberia. Half the livestock was slaughtered, and another severe famine hit in the winter of 1932–33. Millions of peasants poured into the cities, creating new health problems. All in all, it appears that some 4 million people, excluding children, died as a direct or indirect result of collectivization, and the birthrate plummeted.[4] The period of the collectivization drive—that is, of the First Five-Year Plan—was one of great tension for the regime as well as for the population; Stalin was later to tell Winston Churchill that it had been more stressful than World War II.[5]

Paradoxically, as the position of the political system as a whole became more secure in the second half of the 1930s, Stalin launched an unprecedented attack on the political and administrative elite in the purge of 1937–38 (the Great Purge). Western estimates of millions of deaths in the purge seem grossly inflated, but at a minimum tens of thousands died, and likely more.[6] The death rate was some 75 percent among top governmental officials, regional leaders, high military commanders, and directors of the most important factories.

Finally, of course, there was World War II. In the first fifteen

3. Ibid., p. 41.
4. Ibid., pp. 133–37, 140.
5. Winston S. Churchill, *The Hinge of Fate* (Houghton Mifflin, 1950), p. 498.
6. Jerry F. Hough and Merle Fainsod, *How the Soviet Union Is Governed* (Harvard University Press, 1979), pp. 176–77.

months after Hitler attacked the USSR (on June 22, 1941), his army reached the Volga River at Stalingrad and the outskirts of Leningrad and Moscow. Millions died during this advance and more later: the official Soviet estimate of the number of deaths due to the war stands at 20 million—10 million in the military and 10 million civilians.[7] A League of Nations publication projected that the Soviet population in 1950 would have been 225 million had there not been a war;[8] instead the population in 1951 was 182 million.

After the war the Stalinist repression was less deadly, though still severe, in the heartland of the Soviet Union. But the Baltic States, the Western Ukraine, Western Belorussia, and Moldavia, which had been acquired in 1939 and 1940, were subjected to the collectivization and nationalization that the rest of the Soviet Union had experienced in the late 1920s and early 1930s.

The upheavals that Russia went through in the first half of the twentieth century were certainly not limited to the masses; they had an even greater impact on the political elite. The revolutions of 1917 and especially the civil war did more than remove a number of officeholders. They resulted in the almost total elimination of a politico-social stratum, either through death, or, more commonly, emigration. Russian society lost a great proportion of its educated people—especially the most-educated ones.

Similarly, the Great Purge was chiefly aimed at the elite of the time; there is little evidence that many peasants, workers, and lower white-collar employees were killed. Even the highly elite group of listed telephone users in Moscow had a turnover rate from 1937 to 1939 that was only some 6 percentage points higher than it had been from 1935 to 1937.[9] But the impact of the Great Purge on the upper administrative and political elite was devastating. Although these were people who, with few exceptions, had been Stalin's loyal supporters in his struggles against the oppositionists of the 1920s, perhaps 75 percent of the top 1,000 officials in the country were killed in the purge and others were removed from office. The less important one's post in the administra-

7. B.Ts. Urlanis, *Istoriia odnogo pokoleniia* (Moscow: Mysl', 1968), p. 205.
8. Lorimer, *Population of the Soviet Union*, p. 188.
9. Sheila Fitzpatrick, "The Great Purge of 1937–1938: A Statistical Case Study" (University of Texas, 1980). A preliminary calculation established the dropout rate at 11 percent in 1935–37 and 17 percent in 1937–39.

tive hierarchy, the less likely one was to perish, but the removal rate in the top 10,000 political, administrative, and economic posts must have been very high. Some of these people were transferred to low-level work, but, again, if there had been an accumulation of knowledge and experience—this time among the top elite who had come to power in the first years of the Soviet regime—it was lost to the country as completely in 1937–38 as it had been in 1917–21.

The purge had another effect that is even more important for an understanding of the Soviet Union during the last forty-odd years. It involved the destruction not merely of individuals but of a generation: the generation of top officials who had been active in the revolution and the civil war. On the average, the people's commissars (ministers) in 1937 had been born in 1890 and had joined the party in 1910; the top provincial leaders had been born in 1892 and had joined the party in 1912–13. In 1941 these average dates were ten to twelve years later.

The Brezhnev Generation

It is possible to speak abstractly about the impact of a series of events on a "society" over a fifty-year period, but societies are composed of real people who change over time. Those of different ages experience events differently. Wars and major changes in educational systems in particular can create "generations" of young people (or "cohorts," to use the more exact sociological term) whose basic characteristics are determined by their formative experiences. The people who were of the right age to be affected by almost all the events that shook Russia in this century were the generation born between 1900 and 1909—the Brezhnev generation, to name it after its most illustrious representative.

A detailed statistical study has been made of the cohort born in 1906—the year in which, surely not coincidentally, Brezhnev himself was born—and it is a vivid reminder of the nature of Russia at the time. In 1906, 6.2 million babies were born on the territory of what is now the Soviet Union, 89.5 percent of them in rural areas. The infant mortality rate was very high: 1.8 million of these children had died before their first birthday and another 800,000 by the age of five.[10]

10. Urlanis, *Istoriia odnogo pokoleniia*, pp. 76, 94, 114.

The oldest members of the Brezhnev generation received their schooling during the tsarist period and the youngest after the revolution, but many received little education at all. Among those born in 1906, a middle year, 25 percent of the men and 50 percent of the women were still illiterate at the age of twenty. By 1921—when they were fifteen years old—only 5 percent of them had reached the sixth grade. Afterward, many of the 1906 group became enrolled in one or another of the various regime programs to liquidate illiteracy, provide makeup education, establish night schools for adults, and even send adults to college in an affirmative action program. Nevertheless, by 1939 only 12 percent of those born in 1906 could claim to have finished the seventh grade, and by 1959, 61 percent still had had only three years of schooling or less.[11]

The education figures alone show that most of the Brezhnev generation began working at an early age. This of course is the natural thing to happen in the peasant sector of a traditional society during the earliest stages of industrialization, but it was intensified for the members of the Brezhnev generation by World War I. Since many of their fathers and elder brothers were being drafted into the army, there was a great need for hands to help on the farm. This factor was less important for city dwellers; however, the virtual collapse of the economy during the civil war sent people streaming back to the countryside for subsistence. Petrograd (now Leningrad) declined in population from 2,300,000 in 1917 to 740,000 in early 1921.[12]

Although the oldest members of the Brezhnev generation were of an age to fight in either the Red Army or the White armies during the civil war, most of the generation reached adulthood during the 1920s. It was an exciting time. By far the greatest percentage of people continued to work in private farming, but the countryside was often filled with tension because of uncertainty about the regime's future policy and because of the attempts of pro-party activists to change peasant attitudes on such questions as the church, the role of women, and private farming. Many peasants were moving to the cities, either permanently or temporarily, but this migration was slowed by the gradual tempo of reconstruction and fairly high levels of unemployment.

11. Ibid., pp. 125, 134, 136. These figures refer to all citizens of the Soviet Union, including Central Asians. Those for Russians alone are somewhat higher; for example, 85 to 90 percent of the Russian men were listed as literate in the mid-1920s.

12. Lorimer, *Population of the Soviet Union*, p. 188.

Within the intellectual circles, two cultures were in conflict. The professors, the engineers, and the nonadministrative white-collar personnel were rarely party members, and their attitudes were little changed by the revolution. Many had made some peace with the regime in the hope that communism in practice would mean industrialization and modernization, but their general attitude to cultural and social revolution was quite negative. For others, however, the 1920s was a time of experimentation and rebellion. Though often the contents of this rebellion were avant-garde Western rather than Marxist—women's rights, abstract art, sexual revolution, progressive education as proposed by John Dewey, and so forth—many dreamed of creating a Marxist utopia, of overthrowing bourgeois, middle-class values.

Partly for this reason, there were various subgroups among the political and administrative personnel born between 1900 and 1910. Three are particularly important.

The first subgroup was composed of men without any college or specialized education who had entered political work early and stayed on. Some had been junior officers, political commissars, or noncommissioned officers in the civil war and afterward had moved directly into supervisory work. Others were part of a mass recruitment of young workers into the party after Lenin's death. (Most probably, Stalin decided to swamp the party with Russian workers for personal political reasons, believing that they were sufficiently anti-Semitic not to vote for his principal political enemies of the time: Leon Trotsky, Gregory Zinoviev, and Lev Kamenev—all Jews.) Whatever the reasons for the mass admission of workers into the party, they found that membership made them eligible for low-level political and administrative work, and many took advantage of the opportunity.

Members of this subgroup of the Brezhnev generation, however, faced serious obstacles in being promoted to top-level positions. In the 1920s and the 1930s, as has been seen, the important jobs were held by people a decade older who had been active in the party before the revolution and had had an important role in the civil war. In later years the former workers were at a competitive disadvantage with others in their age group who had gone to college.

Nevertheless, after the Great Purge politically (and often physically) wiped out the political and administrative generation that was a decade older, the colleges could not produce enough graduates to fill all the positions being created by rapid industrialization. Consequently, the uneducated subgroup of the Brezhnev generation provided many of the regional party first secretaries, especially in rural provinces, in the 1940s and 1950s (sometimes after some exposure to the Higher Party School in their forties). Moreover a scattering of obituaries of lower-level regional officials suggests that the members of this subgroup may have been the dominant force in the middle and lower reaches of the regional bureaucracy and party apparatus during the 1930s, 1940s, and early 1950s.

The second important subgroup within the Brezhnev generation consists of those who went to college soon after high school. Although the disruptions of the times interfered with the educational process, many of those born between 1900 and 1909 entered college in the early and middle 1920s. Few of these, however, rose to high political and administrative posts in the post–World War II period. (One exception was Georgii Malenkov, Stalin's top lieutenant toward the end of the dictator's rule.) Perhaps some had risen too high by 1937 and were caught in the purge.[13] Perhaps too many went to the social science institutes that, in the 1920s, were considered appropriate for preparation for political leadership, though not by Stalin. (Mikhail Suslov is one man with such a background who rose through party-ideological work.)

Another possibility is that most of the predominantly middle-class graduates of the 1920s went—either by choice or necessity—into science, college teaching, the professions, and lower administrative staff work and avoided both the purge and promotion to high political and administrative posts. Nearly 350 persons born between 1900 and 1909 were subsequently elected full or corresponding members of the USSR Academy of Sciences in recognition of their scientific achievements or of the importance of their post in science administration; they had graduated on the average at twenty-four and seem to have come principally from white-collar backgrounds.[14]

The really important subgroup within the Brezhnev generation—

13. One such example is Konstantin E. Butenko, who graduated from a polytechnical institute in 1927 and was director of the huge Kuznetsk Metallurgical Combine from 1934 to 1937. *Industriia*, November 27, 1937.

14. The biographies of nearly all living and dead members of the Academy of Sciences are published in the *Bol'shaia sovetskaia entsiklopediia* [The Great Soviet Encyclopedia].

including Brezhnev himself—was the product of a conscious decision by Stalin, who had become concerned about the education of the new Communist elite of the 1920s. During Lenin's lifetime, Communists were appointed to the top political posts, and throughout the 1920s this practice was extended to an ever widening number of positions that Westerners consider purely administrative. By 1924, 91 percent of the presidents of the supervisory industrial trusts and 48 percent of the directors of a sample of 639 large factories were members of the party; by January 1926, 78 percent of 770 directors were party members and by 1928, 89 percent.[15] These directors had clearly been appointed not for any technical competency, because in both the 1926 and 1928 samples, more than 75 percent of the directors with party membership had only elementary education, whereas only 3 percent of them had higher education.[16] It was not an accident that the Communist directors had such a low educational level, for almost no one with higher education was in the party at this time. In 1928 only 1.2 percent of the "specialists" employed in the economy (those with higher and specialized secondary education) were party members, and only 0.9 percent of the engineers employed in the industrial enterprises.[17] Most of these party specialists were surely recent college graduates.

In 1922 Lenin expressed his concern about the relationship of the small, uneducated Communist leading core and the non-Communist administrative system it supervised:

Suppose we take Moscow with its 4,700 responsible Communists, and suppose we take that huge bureaucratic machine, that huge pile—who is directing whom? I doubt very much that it can truthfully be said that the Communists are directing this pile. To tell the truth, they are not doing the directing, they are being directed.[18]

Trotsky was even more alarmist. The industrial administration was, in his words, "a cell of world counterrevolutionaries . . . a durable, solid

15. Edward Hallett Carr, *Socialism in One Country* (Macmillan, 1958), vol. 1, p. 109; *Bol'shevik*, April 20, 1928, p. 64.

16. *Bol'shevik*, April 20, 1928, p. 64.

17. T.H. Rigby, *Communist Party Membership in the USSR* (Princeton University Press, 1968), p. 409; I.P. Barmin, *Iz opyta raboty KPSS i Sovetskogo gosudarstva po sozdaniiu kadrov sovetskoi intelligentsii* (Moscow: Izdatel'stvo Moskovskogo universiteta, 1965), p. 9.

18. *Protokoly odinnattsatyi s'ezd rossiiskogo kommunisticheskoi partii (bol'shevikov) stenograficheskii otchet* (Moscow: Izdatel'skoe otdelenie Ts.K.R.K.P., 1922), p. 25.

economic nucleus which leads a struggle against us with weapons in its hands."[19]

There is every indication that Stalin shared these concerns. In the late 1920s he spoke with contempt about the ability of untrained Communists to control their more highly educated and non-Communist subordinates and demanded that the Communists educate themselves. He asserted that "not a single ruling class has managed without its own intelligentsia" and that "the working class must create its own productive-technical intelligentsia."[20]

These beliefs were reflected in the educational policy initiated at that time. Engineering education was emphasized at the expense of the social sciences and the humanities, and the network of engineering institutes and the number of students enrolled in them increased dramatically. Under the First Five-Year Plan (1928–32) a vigorous affirmative action program was launched to change the social composition of the student body. According to official statistics, the percentage of workers and workers' children among college students rose from 20.7 percent in the 1924–25 school year to 26.5 percent in the 1927–28 school year, to 35.2 percent in 1929–30, and to 51.4 percent in 1931–32. In the industrial and transportation technical institutes, the percentage of workers and workers' children had risen to 64 percent in 1931–32.

The most distinctive feature of the First Five-Year Plan affirmative action program was the vigorous recruitment of adults into college. By 1932 fewer than one-third of all students were twenty-three years of age or less, the normal age of graduation. Workers and very low level officials, often ones without high-school diplomas, were being sent to full-time institutes to create the new working-class intelligentsia that Stalin had demanded.[21]

The figures on working-class origin are exaggerated because of the possibility of "obtaining" working-class status (a child of white-collar parents could take a job for several years as a worker) or even acquiring falsified documents, and the dramatic increase in the number of

19. Ibid., p. 136.
20. I.V. Stalin, *Sochineniia* (Moscow: Gospolitizdat, 1951), vol. 13, p. 67. See Sheila Fitzpatrick, "Stalin and the Making of a New Elite, 1928–1939," *Slavic Review*, vol. 38 (September 1979), pp. 377–402; the quotation is from p. 381.
21. Sheila Fitzpatrick, *Education and Social Mobility in the Soviet Union, 1921–1934* (London: Cambridge University Press, 1979), pp. 181–205.

students meant that the white-collar contingent could grow in size even as its relative percentage declined. Nevertheless, the quality of education was strongly affected by the mass influx of ill-prepared students into colleges being expanded far faster than their ability to find qualified instructors. Moreover, during this period a cultural revolution was going on that attacked the traditional nonparty intelligentsia and undercut any effort by professors to maintain former academic standards.

Those who were destined to become important political leaders were no doubt active politically while in college. Brezhnev was at various times in his college career (1930–35) director of the workers' preparatory division, participant in a collectivization group, leader of an antiflood brigade, chairman of the institute trade union, and party secretary of his class.[22] Another student of the time, a future first secretary of the Stalingrad regional party committee, reported that he and other students often missed class because of "ideological flu"—that is, because of various extracurricular assignments.[23]

As suggested in a novel of the 1950s, the consequences of all this activity could be devastating. One of the leading characters, Semen Malinov, a regional first secretary, had graduated from the Bauman Institute, probably the finest engineering school in the country, but his own education did not reflect the excellence of the institution:

Even then Semen Malinov had one main gift—the ability to speak and to imitate. . . . Thanks to such oratorical gifts, Semen Malinov was "loaded" and "overloaded" with assignments: he was one of the Komsomol leaders in the institute, the chairman of the civil defense unit, of the Aid to the Revolutionaries Society, and even of the sports circle. . . . And science? Science remained somewhere at the side. He did not drag himself to the books, and he listened to lectures according to the proverb: "In one ear and out the other." But it was necessary to pass the exams, and Semen Malinov unwillingly had to resort to the method of "dodging." To some teachers he gave his honored word: "I'll hand it in! I'll hand it in! Word of honor, I'll hand it in. Just give me a grade now. . . . I will get it in to you." To others, who were a little sterner, he answered the questions with patter, impudently looking into their eyes. When he did not hit the point, he began to complain about being swamped with work. The "stern" professor would yield, saying "Yes, yes. I know. I know. I've seen your picture in the Komsomol newspaper." . . . And he wrote on the grade

22. *Leonid I. Brezhnev: Pages from His Life* (Simon and Schuster, 1978), pp. 27–29; *Pravda*, December 11, 1976, p. 3.

23. A. Chuianov, *Na stremnine veka* (Moscow: Politizdat, 1976), p. 39.

sheet "Passes." . . . With such dodges [Malinov] left the institute having received the diploma of an engineer, but not the knowledge of one.[24]

In practice, the quality of the education of the First Five-Year Plan subgroup must have varied greatly from person to person. Biographies of prominent figures of the postwar period occasionally report that this or that man had graduated "with distinction" (s otlichiem) and even that he had been involved in technological invention. A number of these graduates went into science and scientific administration and prospered there. On the average, however, the assault on educational standards must have been effective.

Whatever the quality of their education, members of this subgroup were soon thrust upward with dizzying speed during the Great Purge. Those who were admitted to college from 1928 to 1931 graduated, assuming they had not dropped out, from 1932 to 1936. Generally those who were to prosper the most were first assigned to low-level posts in industry (foreman, shop head, or the like) and enjoyed fairly rapid but orderly promotion in the period up to 1937. From 1937 to 1939, however, there was nothing orderly about most of the promotions. A young engineer in a major Leningrad artillery plant could travel to Moscow with the gloomy director of his plant and suddenly, totally unexpectedly, find himself named as the director's successor.[25] A minor Central Committee functionary, who had finished graduate school in 1937, could be named first secretary of the Stalingrad regional party committee so suddenly in early 1938 that he did not have time to go home for a suitcase and had to phone his wife on the way to the station.[26] (Otherwise, no doubt, she would have concluded that it was he who had been purged.) Even promotion through a progression of posts could bring a man to the top quickly. Dmitrii Ustinov, the present minister of defense, graduated in 1934 and became people's commissar of armaments in 1941 at the age of thirty-three. Aleksei Kosygin graduated in 1935 at the age of thirty-one and four years later was people's commissar of the textile industry. When a candidate for promotion protested that he did not have sufficient preparation for his new post, he might be told,

24. Fedor Panferov, *Volga-Matushka reka* (Moscow: Sovetskii pisatel', 1954), pp. 184–86.
25. M.E. Nosovskii, "Pushki na konveire," in I.M. Danishevsky, compiler, *Byli industrial'nye: Ocherki i vospominaniia* (Moscow: Politizdat, 1970), p. 125.
26. Chuianov, *Na stremnine veka*, pp. 42–43.

"After 24 hours we consider a director experienced."[27]

Obviously not every graduate of the First Five-Year Plan subgroup became a minister, a first secretary, or a plant director overnight. Brezhnev himself had only made it to the level of regional party secretary by 1941 (not even second secretary). Those who could not cope with their responsibilities slipped back to lower levels, and others were never thought worthy of major promotion. But, as the gloomy artillery plant director told his young subordinate on the train to Moscow, thirty-three was, indeed, "a good age" in 1937–38.[28] With very few exceptions, the graduates in this subgroup survived the purge. They were promoted at a very young age, had the honor of successfully administering the Soviet economy during World War II, and, as a group, dominated the Soviet administrative system for over twenty years.

The 1910–18 Generation

The 1910–18 generation of politicians and administrators obviously had many experiences in common with their predecessors, and, of course, no clear boundary line exists between 1909 and 1910. But in two important respects a few years could make an enormous difference. First, anyone born after 1910 was too young to be returned to college in the 1928–32 period as an adult, and, second, anyone born much after 1910 was too young to experience a sensational rise during the Great Purge.

In its origins the 1910–18 generation was divided into two subgroups with fairly distinctive experiences. World War I so affected the birthrates that the number of children born annually during the war was some 40 percent lower than in the years before 1915.[29] Perhaps because it was a small group and, more important, because it did not reach the age of admission to first grade (seven years old) until the chaos of the civil war had ended, the post-1914 subgroup was much better educated on a mass level. At the time of the 1959 census, only 18.9 percent of those born between 1910 and 1914 had as much as an incomplete secondary education (not much change from the 15.4 percent of those born

27. *Komsomol'skaia pravda*, February 10, 1938, p.10.
28. Nosovskii, "Pushki na konveire," p. 125.
29. Over 3.6 million a year were born and survived in the period before World War I, as against only 2.6 million a year from 1915 to 1917. The number did not return to prewar levels until 1923. Lorimer, *Population of the Soviet Union*, p. 231.

between 1905 and 1909), but this figure rose to 32.5 percent for those born between 1915 and 1919.[30]

The character of the future elite among the 1910–18 generation was affected less by the difficulties in their early schooling than by what Nicholas Timasheff called "the Great Retreat" of 1931–34.[31] The years 1928–31 had the spirit of Mao Tse-tung's "Great Leap Forward" thirty years later: wildly unrealistic goals, forced collectivization with mass deportation of peasants, a cultural revolution, a vicious attack on religion with a large-scale destruction of churches, a policy of pell-mell party admission that resulted in a tripling of the number of members from January 1927 to January 1933. The theme of all-out class war was carried over into foreign policy, and even moderate socialists were denounced as social fascists, no better than the real fascists and even more dangerous because of their camouflage.[32]

The cultural revolution affected many of the 1910–18 generation in their secondary education. The old secondary school in the 1920s had retained many of its prewar characteristics, including a liberal arts and science curriculum. But then for a few years it was abolished, and replaced by factory schools that were attached to an industrial plant, where production training became an important part of the curriculum. Furthermore, collectivization must have had a devastating effect on rural education, all the more so because it was often accompanied by attacks on the "bourgeois" teachers, who frequently had even more "bourgeois" or "kulak" husbands.

Starting in 1931, the leadership began reversing these policies. It reestablished the secondary school but, even more important for the 1910–18 generation, largely abolished affirmative action programs of college admissions. One could still get an engineering degree by going to evening school for five years, especially if one already worked in industry, but the standards of admission were tightened for entry into full-time day college. The Great Retreat also brought an end to the harassment of professors, and put a renewed emphasis on tougher standards in grading.[33]

30. *Itogi vsesoiuznoi perepisi naseleniia 1959 goda, SSSR (svodnyi tom)* (Moscow: Gosstatizdat, 1962), p. 75.

31. Nicholas S. Timasheff, *The Great Retreat* (Dutton, 1946).

32. Sheila Fitzpatrick, "Cultural Revolution as Class War," in Sheila Fitzpatrick, ed., *The Cultural Revolution in Russia, 1928–1931* (Indiana University Press, 1978), pp. 8–40.

33. Fitzpatrick, *Education and Social Mobility*, pp. 209–33.

Table 3-1. *Class Origins of Officials of the Brezhnev and the 1910–18 Generations*
Percent

Period of birth	Worker	Peasant [a]	White collar [b]
1900–09	45	41	14
1910–18	26	39	35

Source: Elite sample of 1,011 top postwar officials who held the post of USSR minister or deputy minister, secretary or department head of the Central Committee, chairman of the executive committee of the regional soviet, first or second secretary of the regional party committee, or first secretary of the city party committee of the regional capital.

a. Because peasants born between 1907 and 1913 were of a prime age to have their enrollment in college adversely affected by collectivization, only 33 percent of the officials born in those years came from a peasant background, as opposed to 45 percent of those born between 1900 and 1906 and 50 percent of those born between 1914 and 1918.

b. The figures in this table differ considerably from the comparable figures in table 3-3 because (1) there only local officials are included, and (2) here officials with unspecified origins are excluded. The figures here reflect the fact that a higher proportion of ministers and deputy ministers have white-collar origins.

In practice, those of the 1910–18 generation who entered college in the 1930s usually did so within a few years of graduation from secondary school. An elite sample of 1,011 top postwar officials in the center and in the RSFSR regions showed that on the average those born in 1906, 1907, or 1908 had graduated from college at twenty-seven, whereas those born in 1912, 1913, or 1914 graduated at twenty-four.[34] The changing criteria of college admission are also reflected in the higher percentage of officials in the 1910–1918 generation who came from white-collar backgrounds (see table 3-1).

The Great Retreat had another major impact on the 1910–18 generation. During the 1920s, people had often been admitted to the party as early as age twenty, twenty-one, or twenty-two. For future politicians and administrators of the Brezhnev generation, admission to the party often came before admission to college and in many cases led to a college degree that would otherwise not have been obtained. (Seventy-three percent of the officials in the elite sample who were born between 1900 and 1906 and received a full-time college education in the 1930s had joined the party before entering college.) And, as mentioned earlier, the political frenzy of 1928–31 had been reflected in high rates of admission, so that the party had tripled in size from 1927 to 1933.

As part of the Great Retreat, the party leadership summarily stopped all party admission in December 1932 and began weeding out many

34. These figures refer only to those who graduated before World War II. A number of officials in both age groups were sent to the Higher Party School after the war.

of those brought in during the years of easy admission. Western attention has focused on the expulsions because, after four years of bloodless purging, the process turned lethal in its closing phase. In many respects, however, the cessation of admission was also very important. Except for some people born in 1910 and 1911, this new generation of administrators entered the party after college graduation rather than before. In fact, if the wartime years are excluded, the practice of deferring party enrollment until prospective members were in their mid-twenties became general after the Great Purge. The regime wanted to ensure that members were dedicated to the party in deeds as well as words; by postponing the age of membership, it gave candidates the time to demonstrate this dedication in their work. The result for future administrators and politicians was that technical competence became a criterion for party membership rather than the other way around.

The Wartime Generation

Although this generation is difficult to define precisely, in the main it consists of those who entered adulthood just before or during World War II. These are the men who were too young to have acquired the specialized education that would have put them into the defense industry during the war instead of into the army, that is, those who were of prime draft age and who would have been in college in peacetime. In practical terms, a man born in 1916, 1917, or 1918 who had a nondescript career before the war but who rose into command or political work while at the front and then into political and administrative work after the war is also a member of the wartime generation. On the other hand, a man born in 1923, 1924, or 1925 who had limited exposure to the war (often either because of a serious wound early in the war or late entry into it) is much more of the postwar generation, as it is being defined here, at least if he entered college soon after demobilization.

The biographical data suggest that, in general, the men born between 1919 and 1925 were the ones most deeply affected by the war. The first effect was simply one of devastation. The war must have taken a heavy toll among all people who were in their twenties and thirties at that time, but even so the carnage among those born in the first years of the Bolshevik regime was awesome in its scale. The 1959 census found only 10,400,000 citizens who had been born in the 1915–19 period and 11,600,000 in the 1920–24 period, as against 19,000,000 born between 1925 and 1929.[35]

Obviously age groups comprising millions of people have enough members to staff top-level posts that number in the hundreds, or at most in the thousands. And one could imagine a system of veterans' preference in college admissions and hiring that would have brought those engaged in low-level military command and political work during the war to the fore. But two factors worked strongly against the survivors of the wartime generation. The first was the enormity of the reconstructon task and the severe shortage of relatively young manpower, which led the regime to encourage veterans to return to the civilian economy rather than to college. The second was the regime's belief that technical education was the proper preparation for political and administrative careers. (Of those in the elite sample who had been born between 1906 and 1918 and who had received a college education before the war, 70 percent were engineers and 15 percent agricultural specialists.)

The members of the Brezhnev and the 1910–18 generations were still quite young in the first decade of the postwar period, and the engineers and agronomists among them, the majority of whom had spent the war in the defense industry and agricultural administration, were promoted into mainline party and governmental work as openings occurred. The returning veterans who did not have higher education usually moved into positions that seldom led to high-level posts in the government or the party apparatus: ideological and organizational work, the trade union, trade and the services, small light industry and food industry enterprises, and the like. Those who went into lower-level rural work were not competitive with the graduates of agricultural institutes when Khrushchev began emphasizing the improvement of agricultural production instead of simply procurements.

Many in the wartime generation did strive to obtain a college education after the war, but men who had spent years in the military had usually forgotten too much mathematics to compete successfully in the

35. *Itogi vsesoiuznoi perepisi naseleniia 1959 goda, SSSR (svodnyi tom)*, p. 49.

Table 3-2. *Percentage of Postwar Officials Who Completed Full-Time Higher Education, by Period of Birth*

Period of birth	Number of officials	Percentage completing full-time education[a]
1913–16	130	65
1917–20	92	58
1921–25	85	47
1926–29	82	72
1930–37	66	80

Source: See table 3–1.
a. Does not include higher party education.

technical institutes with the teenagers who had spent the war in secondary school. (The colleges of the postwar years retained and even intensified the emphasis upon standards that had been instituted in the mid-1930s.) Therefore, members of the wartime generation gravitated toward colleges where mathematics was less important: social studies and humanities faculties of the universities (for the better students), pedagogical institutes, party schools. This decision put them at a competitive disadvantage with those who had received the more desirable technical education.

The impact of the war on the wartime generation is seen in table 3-2 and especially in figure 3-1, which shows the major variations in the patterns of the years of birth of different types of RSFSR regional (oblast) officials from 1965 through 1977. The only group of officials to be distributed along a normal bell-shaped curve were those engaged in ideological and organizational work: the party secretary for ideological questions, the chairman of the trade union council, the chairman of the people's control committee, the head of the regional education administration, and so forth. The Brezhnev regime has not demanded technical education for these posts and, except for new appointments in the last few years, has tended to fill them with men who had fought in the war, often as political workers, and who had picked up party or correspondence education after the war. There are also many women in this group, for the presence of men at the front gave young women of the wartime generation a special opportunity to enter civilian political

Figure 3-1. *Years of Birth of RSFSR Oblast and Krai Officials, 1965–77* [a]

Number of *obkom* and *kraikom* secretaries (excluding those for ideological questions) [b]
(total 329)

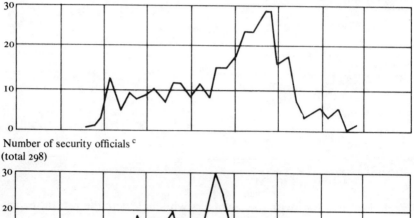

Number of security officials [c]
(total 298)

Number of industry-transportation officials [d]
(total 692)

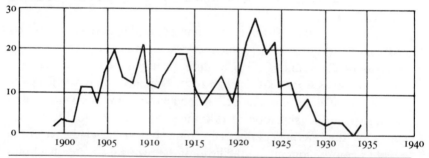

Source: Jerry F. Hough, "The Generational Gap and the Brezhnev Succession," *Problems of Communism*, vol. 28 (July–August 1979), pp. 10–11. The persons included in this sample were identified, and their ages determined, from the lists of deputies to the oblast and krai soviets in 1965, 1967, 1969, 1971, 1973, 1975, and 1977, as drawn from the provincial press. While this methodology does not provide complete coverage of the occupants of the enumerated posts, it does account for an estimated 90 percent of them. Any official who held one of the listed posts at any time during the 1965–77 period and was elected to the oblast or krai soviet in one of the biennial elections is included, but if an official held two posts during the period—for example, moved from head of the agriculture administration to deputy chairman of the *oblispolkom*, or transferred from one oblast or krai to another (applicable only in the cases of KGB and procuracy officials)— he is counted only once.

a. "Oblasts" are regional subdivisions of the union republics; "krais"—of which there are six—differ only in that they contain small nationality units.

b. Including the first secretary, the agricultural secretary, and the two secretaries who divide responsibility for industry, construction, and urban affairs. In earlier years, one of the last two concentrated on organizational matters,

Figure 3-1 *(continued)*

Number of ideological-organizational officials[e]
(total 400)

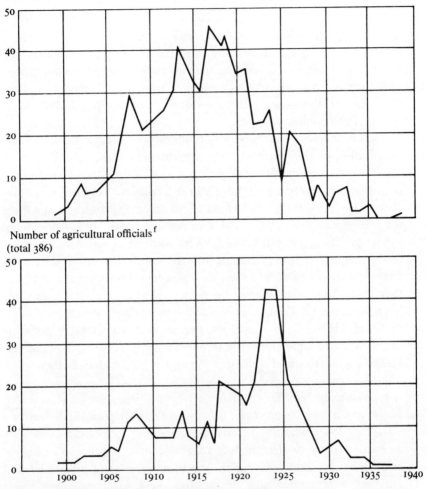

Number of agricultural officials[f]
(total 386)

but that situation has now changed in almost all oblasts and krais.

c. Including the head of the administration of the Committee for State Security (KGB), the head of the internal affairs administration, and the procurator.

d. Including directors of important plants, heads of the railroads and their divisions (*otdeleniia*, which tend to correspond to oblasts and krais), heads of ocean and river steamship lines, and (in 1965 alone) chairmen and deputy chairmen of regional economic councils.

e. Including the *obkom* or *kraikom* secretary for ideological questions, the head of the department of organizational and party work of the *obkom* or *kraikom*, the deputy chairman for education and culture and the heads of the departments of culture and of education of the *oblispolkom* or *kraiispolkom*, the chairman of the oblast or krai trade union council, the oblast or krai newspaper editor, and the chairman of the oblast or krai people's control committee.

f. Including the *obkom* or *kraikom* secretary for agriculture, the deputy chairman for agriculture and the head of the agriculture administration of the *oblispolkom* or *kraiispolkom*, and the chairman of the agricultural supply agency (*Sel'khoztekhnika*).

work, and they tended to go into educational and cultural administration and ideological party work.

Many men of an age to fight in World War II were also selected for law-and-order posts in the RSFSR regions, because here the education that was required was essentially provided by the institution in which the officials were employed. For reasons to be discussed in later chapters, the same pattern is found among top specialists in the international arena—in diplomacy, scholarship, and journalism, as well as, of course, in the military.

Where technical education was required for officials, however, the distribution of the years of birth dramatically shows the impact of World War II. In the first part of the period, the industrial and transportation officials had been largely drawn from the engineering graduates of the 1930s, but as these men began reaching retirement age there were few graduates of the 1940s to replace them. The well-defined trough on the graph marks the missing wartime generation. The relatively small number of graduates from agricultural institutes during the 1930s meant that there were two missing generations in agriculture and that a very high proportion of the personnel selected in this area came from those born in the second half of the 1920s. Because regional party secretaries in the RSFSR, with the exception of the secretary in charge of "ideological" questions, are drawn almost exclusively from graduates of engineering and agricultural institutes, the pattern of their years of birth is quite predictable.

It is conceivable that members of the wartime generation are also distinctive in bearing a crueler burden. A recently published diary of a Soviet engineer who lived through the siege of Leningrad contains a despairing entry, written in July 1942, declaring that the most honest and dedicated, the most daring, the best were being killed and that only the unprincipled and the cowards were surviving. In his 1978 comment on his earlier entry, the engineer repeated his tribute to the fallen, but now he defended the survivors as well.[36] However, the entry itself need not have been published, for it inevitably makes some people aware of a possibility they otherwise may not have considered. Perhaps the purpose of its publication was to provide the occasion for a defense of the survivors against a suspicion that is quite widespread.

36. George Kulagin, *Dnevnik i pamiat'* (Leningrad: Lenizdat, 1978), pp. 246–48.

The Postwar Generation

The fourth generation of politicians and administrators—the postwar generation—consists largely of those too young to have had their college education interrupted by the war (those born after 1925). But the boundary line between the wartime and the postwar generations is indefinite too. A man born in 1924 or 1925 was already somewhat different from one born in 1920: the former had not forgotten as much mathematics by the end of the war and had not had the same opportunity to rise to the type of posts in the army that would qualify him for an immediate administrative or political appointment after the war. A man who was seriously wounded early in the war could also pick up his college education quickly and, in a real sense, be a member of the postwar generation.[37]

At the time of the launching of Sputnik I in 1957, the U.S. media put great emphasis on the high quality of Soviet education as opposed to American education. No doubt, this picture was overdrawn, but it did reflect the fact that educational standards had become rigorous in the Soviet Union in the decade after the war. From the mid-1930s on, education in the regular secondary schools was geared almost exclusively to the college-bound. College admission in turn was very selective, with working class or peasant class origin apparently being given no weight at all; the standards within the colleges were also high.

The future Soviet politicians and administrators who passed through the Soviet colleges at this time bear the mark of this experience as clearly as those who were drawn into higher education in the late 1920s and early 1930s. Many of these older officials had not graduated from a full-time college, and almost none had had a classic pattern of graduation from secondary school, direct entry into a full-time college, and graduation in the normal five years. Even children of white-collar parents had often become industrial workers for a year or two after high school to obtain proletarian status for the purpose of college entry.

By contrast, officials of the postwar generation have relatively few irregularities in their biographies. As seen in table 3-2, the proportion

37. One such example is the Central Committee secretary for industry, V.I. Dolgikh, who was born in 1924, was demobilized from the army in 1943 because of wounds, and then entered an engineering institute.

Table 3-3. *Occupation of Fathers of Key Postwar Local Officials of the RSFSR, by Generation*

Percent

Period of birth	Number of officials	Occupation of father			
		Worker	Peasant	White collar	Unspecified
1900–09	184	40	42	7	11
1910–18	214	27	38	21	14
1919–25	112	13	44	25	18
1926–37	130	18	23	21	38[a]

Sources: Biographies of key officials—those who held the post of regional party first secretary, regional party second secretary, chairman of the executive committee of the regional soviet, or first secretary of the city committee of the regional capital—that were published in the regional press. (Other sources are more random in the way they specify social origin and have been excluded for that reason.)

a. Includes the 5 percent whose parents were listed as "collective farmers"—which probably means that they, as distinct from "peasants," had white-collar jobs on the farm.

of officials in the elite sample with a full, daytime education rose from a low of 47 percent for those born between 1921 and 1925 to 72 percent for officials with 1926 to 1929 birthdates, to 80 percent for those born in the 1930–37 period. Moreover, members of the postwar generation who did enter the daytime division of a college usually did so immediately after high school, or perhaps after a year's preparation for entrance exams or occasionally after a stint in the military. Only 12 percent of the officials who were born in the 1930s and who received full-time degrees are reported to have had a job before college. When there is an irregularity in the biography, it is sometimes more apparent than real. For example, the new Central Committee secretary for agriculture, M.S. Gorbachev, is usually described in Soviet sources as having been an assistant to a combine operator on a farm before entering Moscow University; however, a local biography states that this work was done during the summer while he was going to secondary school.[38]

The class origin of the postwar generation among the important politicians and administrators is more difficult to ascertain, but the trend toward there being more children of white-collar parents—the type of children who do best on rigorous competitive examinations in all countries—seems not only to have continued, but perhaps to have accelerated. As table 3-3 indicates, in the regional press the biographies of officials, which formerly almost always included the occupation of the

38. *Stavropol'skaia pravda*, February 6, 1979.

Table 3-4. *Place of Birth of Key Postwar Local Officials of the RSFSR, by Generation*

Percent

Period of birth	Number of officials	Size of place				
		National capital[a]	One of ten largest cities	One of next largest ninety cities	Smaller town	Village or settlement
1900–09	186	1	4	17	13	65
1910–18	215	2	6	18	14	60
1919–25	106	2	4	16	16	62
1926–37	137	0	2	13	20	64

Source: See table 3-3. Figures are rounded.
a. Until 1917, St. Petersburg, or Petrograd; and Moscow after that.

father of the official, now quite often fail to report this information. Because the second half of the 1920s and the first half of the 1930s saw an enormous movement of peasants into the cities and workers into white-collar jobs, the children born during that period may sometimes have difficulty specifying just how their social origin should be listed. But when more precise information has become available on the occupation of a father of a local official whose social origin had not been listed in a local biography, it almost always turns out to be white collar; consequently, a large number in the unspecified column in the table should be added to the white-collar figures. (This is not so true when no social origin is given in other kinds of sources.)

If the rules of college admission signify that fewer officials came from the lowest levels of society, this should not be taken to mean that the postwar generation of officials was recruited from the top levels. For one thing, the Great Purge undoubtedly had a disastrous effect upon the future careers of the children of the pre-1937 elite. For another, children of the political and administrative elite have tended to go into the professions and especially into scientific research.

In practice, as table 3-4 indicates, 84 percent of the regional elite of the postwar generation were born in villages or small towns (those with a population under 45,000 in 1926). Relatively few biographies of central officials of the postwar generation are available, but they show much the same pattern. Of sixteen top officials in the ministries and the Central Committee apparatus born after 1925, one was born in

Moscow, one in another of the ten largest cities, two in one of the hundred largest cities, four in small towns, and eight in villages.

It is only in an area like science, which attracts many children of the elite, that the statistics have a different appearance. The postwar generation among men elected academicians or corresponding members of the USSR Academy of Sciences—the top scientists and scientific administrators of the country—include 32 percent who were born in Moscow and 18 percent who were born in another of the country's ten largest cities.[39]

The characteristics of the postwar generation that are most visible in short published biographies were determined by the rules of college admission and the educational standards established in the immediate postwar period. But the characteristics—if they exist—that are most important for this analysis were determined as well by the adult experiences of this generation. The Brezhnev generation and the 1910–18 generation spent the heart of their adult lives in the Stalin period, whereas those born in, say, 1928 did not, so that to be successful they had to function effectively in the freer atmosphere of the post-Stalin period. Furthermore, the stage of life at which a person experienced the repudiation of the dogmatic Marxist-Leninist world view of the Stalin years could also have a far more drastic impact than would have been the case if the views on the fundamentals of society had undergone more gradual and imperceptible change.

Obviously there is neither a unanimity of views within a Soviet generation as it has been defined here nor a clean break between the views of different generations. A person's job strongly affects his politically relevant views, and family and other personal life can greatly influence the way he reacts to events. Yet as the generational factor at work is examined in various contexts, it will become even clearer that many aspects of Soviet politics cannot be understood without taking that factor into account.

39. These statistics are based on 102 biographies.

4

The Political and Administrative Elite

To SOME it may seem perverse to discuss generational change among the Soviet elite, let alone to devote a book to it, for the rate of turnover in the ruling Party Politburo and Party Central Committee in recent years has been remarkably low when compared with past Soviet experience. The deaths of Lenin in 1924 and of Stalin in 1953 were both followed by a very visible struggle for power in which the vanquished were removed in disgrace from the country's de facto cabinet, the Politburo. Upon Lenin's death, the Politburo contained seven voting members, but seven years later only one of them—Stalin—remained. The others had been denounced as Left or Right deviationists, and afterward, in the late 1930s, Stalin had them executed as foreign agents. Immediately after Stalin's death, there were ten voting members in the Politburo (then called the Party Presidium), but only two of them—Nikita S. Khrushchev and Anastas I. Mikoyan—remained seven years later. All the rest had been accused of being members of an "antiparty group."

After Khrushchev's removal in 1964, the situation was quite different. The top party body included ten voting members—really nine if one excludes Frol R. Kozlov, who had been incapacitated by a stroke and was removed almost immediately. The two oldest members were retired in 1966, but they had held more or less ceremonial posts. The other seven were still voting members of the Politburo eight years after Brezhnev assumed the general secretaryship. After 1972 the rate of turnover increased; by 1980 three more members of the Khrushchev Politburo and three newcomers elected in 1964–65 were removed and two other newcomers had died. The men who became members in the 1970s, however, were as old on the whole as the men they replaced. The average age of the voting members rose from fifty-eight in 1966 to sixty-two in 1972 to seventy in 1980.

Figure 4-1. *Political Structure of the Soviet Union*

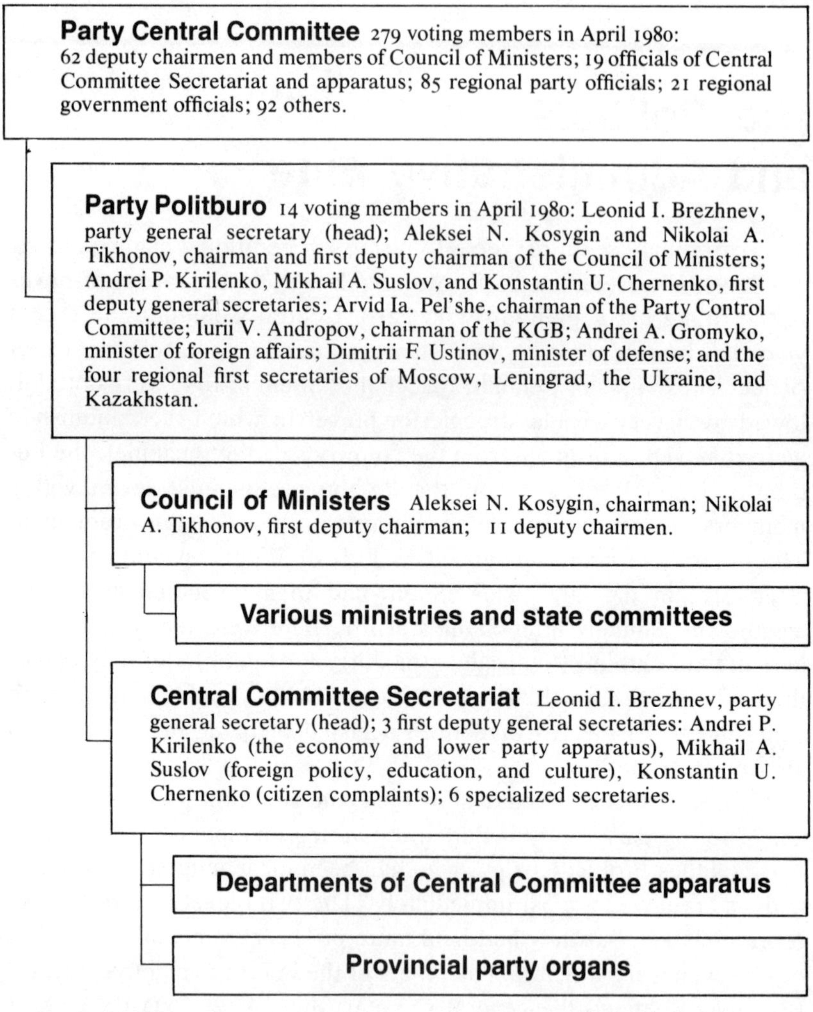

Party Central Committee 279 voting members in April 1980: 62 deputy chairmen and members of Council of Ministers; 19 officials of Central Committee Secretariat and apparatus; 85 regional party officials; 21 regional government officials; 92 others.

Party Politburo 14 voting members in April 1980: Leonid I. Brezhnev, party general secretary (head); Aleksei N. Kosygin and Nikolai A. Tikhonov, chairman and first deputy chairman of the Council of Ministers; Andrei P. Kirilenko, Mikhail A. Suslov, and Konstantin U. Chernenko, first deputy general secretaries; Arvid Ia. Pel'she, chairman of the Party Control Committee; Iurii V. Andropov, chairman of the KGB; Andrei A. Gromyko, minister of foreign affairs; Dimitrii F. Ustinov, minister of defense; and the four regional first secretaries of Moscow, Leningrad, the Ukraine, and Kazakhstan.

Council of Ministers Aleksei N. Kosygin, chairman; Nikolai A. Tikhonov, first deputy chairman; 11 deputy chairmen.

Various ministries and state committees

Central Committee Secretariat Leonid I. Brezhnev, party general secretary (head); 3 first deputy general secretaries: Andrei P. Kirilenko (the economy and lower party apparatus), Mikhail A. Suslov (foreign policy, education, and culture), Konstantin U. Chernenko (citizen complaints); 6 specialized secretaries.

Departments of Central Committee apparatus

Provincial party organs

The Politburo, including the general secretary, is legally responsible to the Central Committee (see figure 4-1). Most of the approximately 280 voting members of the Committee are top party and governmental officials working in the center and provinces;[1] it is they who have the

1. In 1976, 287 voting members were elected, but the number varies as members die and (more infrequently) candidate members are promoted to full membership. For an analysis of the occupations of the members, see Jerry F. Hough and Merle Fainsod, *How the Soviet Union Is Governed* (Harvard University Press, 1979), pp. 456–57.

legal authority to remove Brezhnev and who will have the duty of selecting, or at least ratifying the appointment of, his successor. Although the Central Committee usually seems to make its decisions unanimously, it has the potential to function quite differently from the governmental legislature, the more ceremonial Supreme Soviet. In 1957 the Committee did in fact decide the contest between Khrushchev and his political enemies—the so-called antiparty group.

Since the Central Committee is the principal authority short of the party congresses (which meet periodically and elect the Central Committee), both Stalin and Khrushchev devoted great attention to shaping it in ways favorable to them. In the course of each man's rise to power, he removed many old members from the Committee and expanded its size in order to swamp the survivors by his own supporters. In the Khrushchev era, for example, the voting membership of the Central Committee was expanded 40 percent between 1952 and 1961 (party congresses met in 1956, 1959, and 1961), and only 34 percent of the 1952 voting members still alive in 1961 were reelected to the Committee in that year.

In the Brezhnev era the number of Central Committee voting members was expanded on much the same scale: 46 percent between 1961 and 1971 and a further increase of 19 percent from 1971 to 1976 (party congresses met in 1966, 1971, and 1976). But the old members fared much better. Sixty-six percent of the living members of the 1961 Central Committee were reelected in 1971. Among the core of the voting members of the 1961 Central Committee—the central governmental officials (the deputy chairmen and members of the Council of Ministers), the secretaries and department heads of the Central Committee, the first secretaries of the provincial party committees, and the military officers—79 percent of those still alive were reelected to the Committee a decade later.

In the 1970s the rate of turnover among the Central Committee members managed to decline even further. An incredible 89 percent of the living full members of the 1971 Central Committee were reelected in 1976, and in the four years from early 1976 to early 1980 only 7 to 8 percent of the 1976 Committee members retired or were demoted to posts that are likely to lead to their removal from the Central Committee at the next party congress in 1981. Even though death and the expansion in the size of the Central Committee created some opportunity for rejuvenation, the average age of the voting members (excluding workers and peasants) rose from fifty-two in 1961 to fifty-six in 1966 and to sixty-three in 1980. Because Central Committee members are recruited from among the top party and governmental officials, obviously these latter also tend to be aging.

In some respects Central Committee membership during the Brezhnev era almost took on the appearance of a life peerage—at least members remained until well past normal retirement age.[2] Nevertheless, it would be a mistake to focus on this fact alone and to assume that the rate of personnel turnover is the same throughout the Soviet political system. Even at very high levels, the Central Committee members who have been regional party first secretaries (the top political and administrative officials in the provinces) have often been moved to other posts, so that younger men can be chosen to replace them. In the spring of 1980, the members of the central government who were full members of the Central Committee averaged sixty-six years of age, and the regional first secretaries on that body averaged fifty-eight. Excluding the first secretary, the officials of the Russian regional party bureaus (the provincial equivalent of the Politburo) were on the average fifty-two in early 1980; their counterparts in the Ukraine and Kazakhstan were about a year younger and those in Uzbekistan several years younger. The county party leaders in the Russian Republic were on the average forty-seven.[3]

Because officials at different territorial levels of the country vary so much in age, the pattern of generational change clearly differs from one level to another. The purpose of this chapter is to explore these variations among the mainline political and administrative elite, for the changes that have been occurring there are likely to be reflected in the Central Committee and the Politburo during the next decade.

2. This is not an absolute rule, of course. For example, Alexander Shelepin, a Brezhnev *bête noire*, had been the leader of the Young Communist League. Of fourteen members of the 1961 Central Committee who worked in the Young Communist League from 1948 to 1961 under Shelepin, only one was reelected in 1976, despite the fact they were comparatively younger as a group than other members of the Central Committee.

3. The bureaus were selected in December 1978 and January 1979, and their membership lists were published in the regional papers. The age data on the members (and on county party leaders) were found in the lists of regional deputies published before the June 1977 and February 1980 elections to the local soviets. Information is available on most regions in the Russian Republic and Kazakhstan, but on only seven regions in the Ukraine and three in Uzbekistan.

The Center and the Provinces

In one form or another, conflict between the central government and the local governments is endemic to all modern political systems. But in two respects this relationship in the Soviet Union has ramifications that go far beyond those that Americans would normally anticipate from their own experience.

First, many of the principal territorial units of the country are based on the country's nationalities. The first subdivision of the country—into fifteen union republics—follows the nationality principle, and of course is reflected in the country's official name, the Union of Soviet Socialist Republics. In addition, there are twenty autonomous republics, based for the most part on smaller nationalities, within the huge Russian Republic. As mentioned in chapter 2, the basic nationality group of each republic retains its own language (indeed, the language, usually along with Russian, is the official language of the republic), so that the Soviet Union faces many potential "Quebec" problems. Russians now constitute only 52 percent of the population in the Soviet Union, and because their birthrate is much lower than that of most of the other nationalities, the percentage will continue to decline.

Although the party leadership has so far been successful in controlling unrest in the republics, it remains very sensitive to the nationality issue. No important political decision is made without the nationality component being taken into account. This issue—though often unmentioned—is at the center of all debate about decentralization, economic reform, and, most of all, democratization. In fact, in all three leadership successions to date—Stalin, Khrushchev, and Brezhnev—the man selected as general secretary has been the Politburo member with the most previous experience dealing with non-Russians.

Second, of course, the Soviet system is highly centralized—that is, all political and administrative units in the country are ultimately responsible to the Politburo in Moscow—and in a particular way. In each region the political leaders, both the bureau of the local party organs and the executive committee of the local soviets (similar to the Council of Ministers), are subordinated to the next higher territorial level, but they by no means have sole authority over the specialized administrators within the region.

When Soviet officials and scholars talk about their political system, they frequently refer to the "verticals" and the "horizontals" and the politics within and between them. The verticals are the giant specialized ministerial complexes in Moscow and the lines of command extending vertically down into the provinces. The horizontals are the party and soviet (government) organs in each republic, region, city, and county, which try to coordinate and influence the multitudinous representatives of the verticals in their area. Almost all local administrators are subject to a complex system of dual subordination, one supervisory body being the higher territorial level in the ministerial line of command and the other the local party and frequently soviet organs.

This system of dual subordination (and it officially bears that title) causes some of the major political cleavages in the system. The most prevalent type of conflict involving the regions is that between different territorial units, especially as they compete for funds. Operating funds tend to be distributed by some central formula, but new capital construction and new programs must be financed in a competitive process. Provincial governments do not have a lump sum at their disposal that they then distribute among competing local agencies; instead, each local department appeals to its ministerial line of command for appropriations. Even much of the housing and local services are financed through the industrial ministries that allocate money to their local plants. In this process each of the local claimants usually has the support of local party and soviet officials behind its requests, for its real competitors tend to be the specialized administrators from other areas.

For the future of the Soviet political system, however, the conflicts among the regions are not as important as those that arise from their common frustrations over central control. Although the need to clear all significant investment programs and new programs with Moscow is obviously an irritant, Soviet press articles suggest that the greatest anger arises from the control of housing and service funds among so many individual central ministries, for this plays havoc with local attempts to engage in balanced city planning and to distribute housing and services equitably to all citizens. (The employees of the wealthier heavy industry ministries receive more than those of ministries with fewer financial resources.)

These resentments are perhaps intensified by the feeling that the central officials do not understand the provincial point of view and have had few opportunities to learn about it. The provincial secretaries really are men of the provinces. If study in the Higher Party School in Moscow in mid-career is excluded, only 16 percent of the republican and regional first secretaries in 1974 had been educated in Moscow or Leningrad, and very few (other than the local officials of these cities) had worked there.[4] Particularly in the Brezhnev era, their careers have usually featured promotion within one or two regions rather than movement around a number of regions as the agent of the central leader.[5]

Because regional first secretaries are required to coordinate many specialized activities, they will normally have held jobs both as generalists and as specialists. For example, a first secretary in a heavily urbanized region will usually have had experience in industrial management and urban party work, and a first secretary in a more rural area will usually have worked in agricultural administration and rural party work. Yet before becoming regional first secretaries, both will probably have been moved into general coordinating posts at lower levels either in the city or in the country.

By contrast, the top ministerial officials in the Soviet Union have not normally been political generalists and tend to be more Moscow-centered in their careers. Only 9 percent of the deputy chairmen and members of the Council of Ministers in January 1980 were born in Moscow or Leningrad, but 54 percent received their college education there. (This figure has been gradually declining in recent decades and stood at 85 percent of the college graduates among the 1950 officials.) And most have worked in Moscow for a long time—twenty-four years on the average.

Unlike the practice in most Western countries with a parliamentary system, the top ministerial officials in the Soviet Union do not move from one ministerial portfolio to another, but as a rule have risen within the professional sector—usually the ministry—that they now lead. In early 1980, only twenty-one of the ninety-four deputy chairmen and members of the Council of Ministers had formerly been regional first or second secretaries, and ten of them worked in agriculture, construc-

4. Calculated from the biographies in *Deputaty Verkhovnogo Soveta SSSR, Deviatyi sozyv* (Moscow: Izdatel'stvo "Izvestiia," 1974).

5. T.H. Rigby, "The Soviet Regional Leadership: The Brezhnev Generation," *Slavic Review*, vol. 37 (March 1978), pp. 12–14.

tion, or security, where the role of the regional party committees is particularly great.

The difference in the experiences of the central and regional leaders is accompanied by a great difference in their ethnic backgrounds. The provincial first secretaries in the Russian Republic are normally Russians by nationality, but those in the other republics are almost always men of the local nationality. In 1974, the last year for which full data are available, the 166 republican and regional first secretaries of the Soviet Union consisted of 98 non-Russians and 68 Russians. By contrast, 75 percent of the deputy chairmen and other members of the Council of Ministers were Russian in that year.

Another major institutional center of expertise and political power in Moscow employs top officials with somewhat more provincial experience—the secretaries and employees of the departments of the Central Committee. One of the most distinctive features of the Soviet political system is that committees of the governing party have the ultimate authority in policymaking and that they have a specialized staff that duplicates the governmental structure on a miniature scale to provide them with assistance in this role. Imagine that the Democratic National Committee and its executive committee were the top policymaking bodies in the United States under a Democratic administration. Imagine that the committee had a staff of some 1,500 specialists who were organized into departments such as science and education, heavy industry, agriculture, culture, and administrative organs (police and the military) and that the head of this staff (who would be given the title of general secretary) was the real national leader instead of the President. Such is the character of the Central Committee, its executive committee (the Politburo), and its staff in the Soviet Union.

Although the general secretary and his top lieutenant for general coordination and personnel selection have always had a nonspecialized background (normally including experience as a regional first secretary), most Central Committee officials have backgrounds almost as specialized as those of the ministers. They usually have the college education and work experience appropriate for their particular department and, in fact, were often drawn into party work from administrative or economic work within one of the ministerial hierarchies they now oversee. Thus the head of the chemical industry department of the Central Committee in early 1980 was formerly a deputy minister of the chemical industry; the head of the construction department once headed a construction trust; the head of the transportation department had been a head of a railroad; the head of the foreign personnel department was a former ambassador and then deputy minister of foreign affairs; and the head of the international information department came to his post from the directorship of Tass (the Soviet equivalent of the Associated Press and the United Press International).

The Development of a Generational Gap

For the purposes of this study, the most interesting difference between the top central and top regional officials is the substantial generational gap that has developed between them. In the past this gap did not exist. In 1950 Stalin—born in 1879—was a decade older than all but three high party and governmental officials, and the Politburo members other than Stalin—who were born in 1896 on the average—were approximately a decade older than the political and administrative elite they supervised. This elite, however, was extraordinarily homogeneous in its age distribution. Eleven of the most important governmental officials were born in 1895 or earlier, but the other fifty members of the Council of Ministers (that is, essentially the central government ministers) were born in 1904 on the average, and there was little difference in age between these ministers and even top regional officials (see tables 4-1 and 4-2). On the whole, the Brezhnev generation that had been pushed up during the Great Purge was being retained in high posts rather than being replaced by younger men.[6]

The victory of Khrushchev brought several important changes in the composition of the top political elite. First, Khrushchev, who was born in 1894, declined to surround himself with men of his own generation—that is, men in their sixties. With the exception of two men in their seventies and the very brief experiment with Marshal Zhukov (born in 1896), the seventeen additions to voting membership of the Politburo during the Khrushchev years were born in 1907 on the aver-

6. Only three of the eleven older governmental officials had graduated from college, and none was an engineer. By contrast, almost all the other members of the government were members of the Brezhnev generation in every sense. Eighty-five percent were college graduates, and approximately 80 percent of the graduates were engineers.

Table 4-1. *Average Age of Top Central and Regional Officials, 1950–80*[a]

Officials	March 1950	January 1957	January 1962	June 1966	April 1971	March 1980
General secretary	70	62	67	59	64	73
Other voting members of the Politburo	55	59	59	57	60	69
Central Committee secretaries and department heads[b]	n.a.	49	53	52	57	64
Deputy chairmen of the Council of Ministers	51	56	56	54	59	66
Other members of the Council of Ministers[c]	46[d]	51	54	57	60	65
First secretaries, regional (oblast) party committees	43[e]	47	48	49	51	55

Source: Individual biographies from a variety of Soviet sources.
n.a. Not availalble.
a. The average age is determined by subtracting the average year of birth from the year before the one in the column head. Since a man born in 1910 is only forty-nine on January 1, 1960, and since all columns refer to the first part of the year, it was decided to follow that rule consistently.
b. Excluding the general secretary.
c. For the most part, ministers and chairmen of state committees.
d. This figure excludes one minister, ten years older than the rest, who had been totally incapacitated by a stroke.
e. RSFSR only.

Table 4-2. *Average Age of USSR Council of Ministers and Regional Officials in the RSFSR, 1950–80*[a]

Officials	March 1950	March 1955	March 1961	March 1963	June 1966	June 1971	June 1975	March 1980
Members of the USSR Council of Ministers[b]	46	51	53	54	57	60	62	65
First secretaries, regional (oblast) party committees	43	47	50	49	52	52	54	57
Other secretaries, regional party committees	41	43	46	43	46	47	49	50
Chairmen, executive committees, regional soviets	43	47	49	46	48	50	51	52
Department heads, regional soviets[c]	44	46	48	47	49[d]	49	50	51
First secretaries, city party committees of regional capitals	41	43	45	43	43	44	46	48

Source: Lists of deputies of forty-nine regions (oblasts and krais), published in the regional newspapers at the time of the election.
a. The average age is determined by subtracting the average year of birth from the year before that in the column head.
b. Excluding deputy chairmen of the Council of Ministers.
c. The figures are based on thirteen departments and administrations: agriculture, communal economy, consumers' services, culture, education, finance, food industry, health, internal affairs, local industry, planning, road construction, and trade.
d. Average age in June 1965.

age. If the members of the antiparty group on the Council of Ministers in January 1957 are excluded, the average Council of Ministers official was born in 1905, the average Central Committee secretary and department head in 1907, and the average regional party first secretary in 1909.

Second, the age distribution within the political and administrative elite became considerably more differentiated during the Khrushchev era. Khrushchev spoke repeatedly about the rotation of personnel and the need to promote the young. Almost yearly he conducted a major reorganization somewhere within the central or provincial party and governmental hierarchies, and—to use a cliché of the Brezhnev era— he showed very little "respect for cadres." Officials were not only bounced around in the many reorganizations, but they were quite likely to become the scapegoats for some policy failure and be demoted.

Yet despite Khrushchev's frequent administrative shake-ups and his talk about youth, the age of the central governmental officials increased. In January 1957—before the industrial ministries were abolished and their personnel dispersed, before the Council of Minister officials of the antiparty group within the Politburo were defeated and the protection they afforded the officials beneath them was removed— the average member of the Council of Ministers was fifty-one. In January 1964, after seven years during which Khrushchev was at the height of his power, actually served as chairman of the Council of Ministers, and had carried out a series of reorganizations in the center, the average age of these officials rose to fifty-four.

It was at the lower levels that younger officials were being brought in. In 1960 and 1961 Khrushchev conducted a purge of the lower party apparatus, which caused first secretaries to be changed in 57 of the 101 regions and autonomous republics of the Russian Republic and the Ukraine. With few exceptions the new first secretaries were selected from the 1910–18 generation; the average year of birth of all regional first secretaries went from 1909 in early 1957 to 1913 in early 1962.

But the real impetus to generational rejuvenation of the provincial political elite came with Khrushchev's plan in late 1962 to split both the party organization and the soviets into two in the major regions, one for the urban areas and one for the rural areas. For example, instead of the province—or state, in American terms—of Sverdlovsk having one "governor," one education department, one finance department, and so forth, it now had two of each, and they were administratively independent of each other. Whatever the administrative reasons for this reorganization (and, as can be imagined, it created enormous difficulties), it required a great expansion in the number of top officials in each region. Many of the new appointees were quite young. The rejuvenation of the early 1960s did not mean a mass replacement of officials by a group five years younger, but a more selective replacement in which the new officials were much more than five years younger. The proportion of the regional party first secretaries in the Russian Republic who were from the wartime generation rose from 5 percent to 25 percent between 1961 and 1963. Among regional secretaries other than the first secretary, the breakthrough of the postwar generation was occurring. Twenty-eight percent of these officials were in their thirties in 1963.

In short, an age difference between central and provincial officials began to open up during the Khrushchev years. The striking thing about the Brezhnev succession was that this process continued. In previous successions the general secretary quite soon removed others of his generation from most of the seats on the Politburo and from the ministerial and party apparatus portfolios in Moscow. In 1950 (under Stalin) the average minister was eleven years younger than the average Politburo member and twenty-three years younger than the general secretary. In 1962 (under Khrushchev) these differences were eight and thirteen years respectively. But Brezhnev chose his top lieutenants chiefly from his own generation. This fact became increasingly noticeable as time went on.

In 1966, two years after Brezhnev came to power, the Politburo voting members averaged fifty-seven years of age, virtually the same as the figures of fifty-six in January 1950 and fifty-eight in January 1960. The other high officials in Moscow were older than in the past, though the age distribution among them was quite normal by Western standards. And if those appointed to top jobs are to have gained experience and been tested in a series of increasingly responsible jobs, then those at middle levels of the bureaucracy and party apparatus in the provinces certainly should be younger than the highest officials in Moscow.

The anomaly in 1966, if there was one, came from the backgrounds of the ministers and other members of the Council of Ministers. In the Soviet Union of 1966, men of fifty-seven (the average age of members) had had very diverse career patterns. The abolition of the industrial ministries by Khrushchev had forced many ministerial personnel into the provinces and had given many local officials a fresh opportunity to rise. But few of the latter made it to the top after 1965. The same is true of nearly all the former ministerial officials who spent more than a few years in the regional council outside Moscow. The new chairman of the Council of Ministers, Aleksei Kosygin, had become a minister in 1939 and a deputy chairman of the Council of Ministers in 1941, and many of those with whom he surrounded himself had worked in Moscow for years.

Brezhnev's preference for familiar faces in the center was dramatically confirmed later: during the 1970s the rate of personnel change at the top was remarkably sluggish. Of the sixty-eight members of the Council of Ministers (including deputy chairmen of the Council of Ministers) in 1966, only eighteen had retired or been removed by the spring of 1980—fourteen years later—despite the fact that the survivors then averaged seventy years of age. Similarly, only six of the twenty-three Central Committee secretaries and department heads named after the Twenty-third Party Congress in 1966 had retired or been removed to a lesser post during that period.

To some extent these statistics overstate the stability of personnel. The fact that the Brezhnev regime has tolerated Parkinsonian tendencies throughout the political system (reflected, for example, in an increase in the number of ministries from forty-seven in 1966 to sixty-three in 1980 through a process of subdivision) has permitted the appointment of many new officials. Moreover, fifteen of the members of the Council of Ministers and two of the Central Committee secretaries and department heads died in office during this period, almost as many as the number who retired or were removed. Nevertheless, by early 1980 the average age of the deputy chairmen of the Council of Ministers had risen to sixty-six, that of other members of the Council of Ministers to sixty-five, and that of Central Committee secretaries and department heads to sixty-four.

The situation in the provinces was quite different. As tables 4-1 and 4-2 show, some aging has occurred among the regional first secretaries—the top leaders in each of these territorial units—but below that level the increase in average age has been relatively slight in the Brezhnev era. With the reunification of both the lower party apparatus and local soviets in 1965, the average ages returned to about the 1961 level,

Table 4-3. *Age Distribution of RSFSR Regional Officials, 1980*

Percent, except for average age

Age and period of birth	Regional party first secretaries	Other regional party secretaries	Chairmen, regional soviets	Department heads, soviets
Under 40 (after 1939)	0	2	0	4
40–44 (1935–39)	0	18	8	12
45–49 (1930–34)	20	24	27	19
50–54 (1925–29)	25	34	41	36
55–59 (1920–24)	16	13	14	21
60–64 (1915–19)	25	8	8	7
65 and over (pre-1915)	13	1	2	1
Average age	57	50	52	51

Sources: The age data are drawn largely from reports of nominations of candidates for regional soviets, January–February 1980, in thirty-seven regions for which such data were published in the regional press. Other sources are available for regional party first secretaries and chairmen of the executive committees or regional soviets, and those percentages are based on fifty-five regions. Figures are rounded.

Table 4-4. *Average Age of RSFSR Regional Officials of Different Sectors, 1965, 1973, and 1980*

Sector	1965	1973	1980
Agriculture[a]	45	46	49
Industry[b]	47	48	50
Trade and services[c]	48	50	52
Ideological-educational[d]	45	50	52
Law and order[e]	48	51	53
Control[f]	47	53	55

Source: Reports in the regional press of birth dates of nominees for deputies to regional soviets.

a. The officials included are the regional party secretary for agriculture, the deputy chairman of the executive committee of the regional soviet for agriculture, the head of the agriculture administration of the regional soviet, and the head of the agricultural machinery supply agency.

b. The officials included are the two regional party secretaries who handle urban affairs and the heads of the local industry administration and the food industry administration of the regional soviet.

c. The officials included are the deputy chairmen of the executive committee of the regional soviet for trade and consumer goods, the head of the trade administration and the head of the consumers' services administration of the regional soviet, and the chairman of the consumers' cooperatives (the rural trading agency).

d. The officials included are the regional party secretary for these questions, the deputy chairman of the executive committee of the regional soviet for education and culture, the editor of the regional newspaper, and the head of the education department and the head of the culture administration of the regional soviet.

e. The officials included are the chairman of the KGB, the regional prosecutor, and the head of the internal affairs administration of the regional soviet (the head of the regular police).

f. The officials included are the chairmen of the people's control committee and the head of the finance department of the regional soviet.

for often the younger of two parallel officials in the urban and rural organs became the deputy of the older. Even with this tendency, however, the difference between the 1963 and 1966 averages was never more than three years—just what would have occurred if the same people had retained their offices throughout.

As table 4-2 indicates, the period 1966-71 saw little aging among the provincial elite. Then in the nine years from 1971 to 1980, the average age of the key local party officials (the secretaries of the regional party committees and the first secretary of the capital city party committee) increased by three to four years, and the average age of the top provincial governmental officials rose even less. Except for some of the regional party first secretaries, almost none of these officials is past the American retirement age of sixty-five, and few are even past the official Soviet retirement age of sixty (see table 4-3). Moreover, the average ages are lower and the rejuvenation more thoroughgoing among the officials dealing with the economy—precisely those who are most likely to be promoted to the highest regional posts (see table 4-4).

The Central-Regional Generation Gap and the Succession

The difference in age between the central governmental and party officials on the one hand and the regional officials on the other is an interesting fact in its own right. It demonstrates that petrification in personnel selection has not extended into the provinces and that an ample pool of experienced people are available for promotion if a future leadership so desires. This age difference has, however, a further significance that may be much more important.

In the way in which the leader is selected, the Soviet system is a parliamentary one, in which the parliament, the cabinet, and the prime minister are located in the institutions of the ruling party. The Secretariat and the Politburo (the "cabinet") are subordinated to the Central Committee (the "parliament"), which has the right at any time either to elect or to remove a member of either body, including the general secretary (the "prime minister") himself. (The widespread Western notion that the Soviet Union does not have an institutionalized mechanism for handling the succession is as wrong as it would be for Great Britain.)

What must be kept in mind is that the provincial party and government officials constitute the largest voting bloc in the Central Committee (44 percent in 1976) and that the party officials are a peculiarly important link in the process by which the leadership is selected. The Communists in their primary party organizations (formerly, cells) elect delegates to district and city party conferences. The latter elect delegates to regional conferences, which elect delegates to the national party congress. The congress in turn elects the Central Committee, which, as mentioned before, elects the Politburo and the Secretariat. On paper, the selection procedures inside the party seem democratic; in practice, the votes at each stage of this process are taken unanimously.

Yet it would be wrong to treat the political mechanisms by which a leader is chosen as meaningless. The 280-person Central Committee is at a minimum the institution that must ratify changes of the general secretary and Politburo members; in 1957, at least, this was far from a formality in the showdown battle between Khrushchev and his opponents. The Central Committee membership is itself changed at a party congress, and, though the election votes there are now apparently unanimous, the resulting changes in the composition of the membership can be very significant. The delegates are not freely elected at the provincial conferences, but they do come from the provinces and somehow have to be selected. In practice, the provincial first secretary seems to have de facto control over his provincial delegation; at the congress itself the first secretaries meet prior to the election of the Central Committee to examine the slate of candidates. It is worth noting that in the year after Khrushchev's removal the regularly scheduled party congress was postponed for a number of months, and then soon before it took place, Brezhnev's two main rivals—Nikolai V. Podgorny and Alexander N. Shelepin—were moved into much less powerful posts. Even though the votes of the congress were to be unanimous, the various candidates seemed to be adjusting to what the votes would show if a free ballot had been called.

Indeed, it has been precisely this electoral system that has been the main source of power of the general secretary over the years. The Secretariat, over which the general secretary presides, has the prime responsibility of supervising the local party organs to ensure that central decisions are carried out, and has substantial authority over personnel selection to give force to its directives. Since provincial party secretaries are in a position to control the delegations to the party congresses, they not surprisingly have supported the official in charge of evaluating their work, the man who may have been instrumental in selecting them in the first place. There has therefore been what Robert Daniels has called "a circular flow of power."[7] The general secretary has been able to build a political machine among the provincial party secretaries that gives him control over the party congress. This control in turn has permitted him to stack the Central Committee (including, as has been seen, many more regional officials) and thereby to dominate both the institution that is supposed to control him (that is, the Central Committee) and the Politburo, which is responsible to the Central Committee.

In this process, however, the provincial first secretaries should not be considered mindless robots; particularly during a succession struggle, an intelligent general secretary will try to solidify his support among them by accommodating some of his policies to their interests. In the 1920s Stalin supported their pleas for a dominant role in the economic decisionmaking within the region. In the mid-1950s Khrushchev abolished the industrial ministries and replaced them by regional economic councils that were supervised by the provincial party organs. Brezhnev promised (and delivered) a policy of relative personnel stability, usually giving regional first secretaries that were removed a job of equal status. At times his policies have seemed designed at least in part for their political effect. In 1974, for example, he launched a major investment program for the non–Black Earth areas; two years later a number of regional secretaries from those areas were promoted from candidate membership to full membership in the Central Committee.

As one examines the situation at the beginning of the 1980s, it becomes apparent that the age difference between the central and the regional officials may be of critical importance. If a party congress had been held in 1979, only 32 percent of the delegates would have been chosen from oblasts and small republics whose first secretary was over sixty years old at the beginning of the year. Approximately 19 percent of the delegates would have been from areas where the first secretary was between fifty-six and sixty, 26 percent from areas where he was

7. Robert V. Daniels, "Soviet Politics since Khrushchev," in John W. Strong, ed., *The Soviet Union under Brezhnev and Kosygin* (Van Nostrand-Reinhold 1971), p. 20.

fifty-one to fifty-five, and 23 percent from where he was fifty or younger.[8] Many of these men must be impatient for promotion. Although
there are cleavages among them, a man of the 1910–18 generation
would have support of his own from some of the older Central Committee members to add to that which he could pick up from younger regional secretaries by promising change. Since most kinds of economic
reform would increase the role of local officials in investment decisions and provide the occasion (or excuse) for removing most of the
old industrial ministries, the younger regional secretaries may have a
double reason for supporting a leader who promises change.

8. Lists of all the delegates to the Twenty-fifth Party Congress, together with the
names of the party organizations from which they were elected, may be found in XXV
s"ezd Kommunisticheskoi partii Sovetskogo Soiuza (24 fevralia–5 marta 1976 goda),
Stenograficheskii otchet (Moscow: Politizdat, 1976), vol. 2, pp. 329–596. A tedious process of counting provides the number of delegates elected from each region, and the ages
of first secretaries were determined from the various biographical sources cited in this
book. The ages of new secretaries electing 6 percent of the delegates could not be determined. Half of these were assigned to the fifty to fifty-five group and half to the fifty and
below group.In any case, the figures in the text are only approximations, for geographical migration of the population and differences in the recruitment of new party members
result in marginal changes in the number of delegates elected from each region from congress to congress.

5

The Military

IN MANY respects the pattern of generational turnover among the military over the years is similar to the pattern within the civilian sector. Virtually the entire top military command was wiped out in the Great Purge of 1937–38 and replaced by a less-experienced but better-educated cadre that carried the country through the war. In early 1980 a seventy-one-year-old minister supervised deputy ministers who averaged sixty-four years of age and "regional" officials (the commanders of military districts) who averaged fifty-five.

Yet in a number of ways the military has been different. The top military elite that emerged after the purge was older than the Brezhnev generation that emerged in the civilian sphere, for Stalin had been careful not to kill off all his officers who had fought in the First World War (men born before 1900). Then, after World War II, because victorious generals undoubtedly seemed more threatening to Stalin than their civilian counterparts, many of the top wartime military leaders were fairly quickly moved into lesser jobs—at least until after Stalin died.

The younger military generations, too, were affected by World War II differently from the civilians. For the former, the war was not a great disaster that prevented them from obtaining technical education but their best "school." But those born after 1927, whatever the quality of their military education, have never had the experience of significant military action, and this lack has prevented their moving into high-level positions.

The Purge and the War

The Great Purge had a devastating impact on the armed forces. According to the count of one higher officer who himself was arrested but who survived the camps, 3 of the 5 marshals, 3 of the 4 first-rank army commanders, all 12 of the second-rank army commanders, 60 of the 67 with the rank of corps commander, 136 of the 199 with the rank of division commander, and 221 of the 397 with the rank of brigade commander were arrested.[1] Though some lived through the ordeal, most were shot. By 1939 a new group staffed nearly all the top posts in the military establishment.

At the beginning of 1937, on the eve of the purge, the top seven officials of the Commissariat of Defense averaged only forty-five years of age and the 12 commanders of military districts only forty-four. All but three had joined the party by 1919 and all had had major commands in the Red Army during the civil war. Since the purge was to decimate the top administrative personnel in all walks of life, these men, like many others, were in terrible danger in early 1937. But they also had two special marks against them. First, they had served directly under Trotsky, who was the leader of the army (the commissar of defense) during the civil war. Second, the clandestine arrangements on military training between the Soviet Union and Weimar Germany during the 1920s had given many of them personal contacts with the German military. Indeed, only two of the eighteen commanders were still alive in 1939.

Although the fate of the top military officers had much in common with that of the leading civilian administrators, the characteristics of the successors of the two groups were dissimilar in important ways. As has been seen, in 1941 most of the members of the Politburo and the deputy chairmen of the Council of People's Commissars (as the Council of Ministers was then called) were essentially of the same age as those who had died in the purge, but almost all the men at the next level down—the people's commissars (ministers) and the regional party first secretaries—were of a different generation—the Brezhnev generation. The great majority had been born between 1898 and 1907, had received college education in the Soviet period after entering college as adults, and had risen precipitously during the purge.

The top military leaders of 1941, by contrast, were nearly a decade older than their civilian counterparts and were actually older than their own predecessors had been four years earlier (see table 5-1). The eight most important military officials—the deputy chairman of the Council of People's Commissars and chairman of the Defense Committee (Kli-

1. Roy A. Medvedev, *Let History Judge: The Origins and Consequences of Stalinism* (Knopf, 1971), p. 213.

Table 5-1. *Average Year of Birth of Top Civilian and Military Officials, 1937 and 1941*[a]

Post	January 1937	1941[b]
Civilian commissars (ministers)[c]	1891	1901
	(16)	(26)
First secretaries, regional (oblast) party committees	1892	1903
	(20)	(11)
Commissars, deputy commissars, and chief of staff, Commissariats of Defense and (in 1941) Navy	1890	1893
	(7)	(14)
Other high commissariat officials	1887	1898
	(9)	(12)
Commanders of military districts (before the war)	1892	1895
	(12)	(11)
Commanders of fronts (June–December 1941)[d]	. . .	1895
		(15)
Commanders of armies (June–December 1941)[d]	. . .	1896
		(42)

Sources: *Sovetskaia voennaia entsiklopediia* [The Soviet Military Encyclopedia], vols. 1–6 (Moscow, 1976–78); *Bol'-shaia sovetskaia entsiklopediia* [The Great Soviet Encyclopedia], 30 vols.; and biographies and obituaries in the military newspaper *Krasnaia zvezda* [Red Star] from 1956 to the present.

a. The figures in parentheses indicate the number of officials included in each group.

b. For the civilian officials, 1941 means May 1941. For the commanders of military districts, it means January 1, 1941. For other military categories, it means an official identified in the category at any point during the period in question; hence there is a small overlap in the figures when a man moved from one category to another.

c. This category excludes a small number of commissars who were also deputy chairmen of the Council of People's Commissars.

d. A front was the most important military fighting unit and included a number of armies, usually about four. An army was subdivided into corps, which were subdivided into divisions, and so forth.

ment E. Voroshilov), the commissar of defense (Semen K. Timoshen-ko), and his six deputy commissars—were with one exception a most unimpressive group. That exception, Boris M. Shaposhnikov, had been a colonel in the tsarist army and a high official in the Soviet army (chief of staff and later commander of the Leningrad military district) who had survived the purge. However, the other seven had all come out of one fighting unit during the civil war, the First Cavalry Army, whose commander had been Semen Budenny and whose top political officer had been Voroshilov, a close associate of Stalin's. None of the First Cavalry group had obtained a higher military education after the civil war. Born in 1890 on the average, they gave every appearance of having been selected for their political connections. The leadership of the Naval Commissariat was more professional, as were three new

Table 5-2. *Educational Background of Top Military Officers, 1937 and 1941*

Percent

Post	Number of officers	Type of higher military education[a]		
		Tsarist	Soviet	None
January 1, 1937				
Commissar, deputy commissars, and chief of staff	14	43	14	43
Other high commissariat officials	9	56	22	22
Commanders of military districts	12	33	8	58
June–December 1941				
Commissars, deputy commissars, and chief of staff, Commissariats of Defense and Navy	14	14	50	36
Other high commissariat officials	11	0	91	9
Commanders of fronts	15	0	87	13
Commanders of armies	40	3	55	42

Sources: See table 5-1. Figures are rounded.

a. "Tsarist" almost always means an *uchilishche*—a military school that one entered immediately after secondary school or while a young soldier. (Strictly speaking, this is not higher education, but secondary.) "Soviet" almost always means a mid-career academy for men already officers and usually involves a three-year term of study. Nearly all these officers have also gone through various courses of preparation that may last up to a year. If this was the only military education an officer received, he is listed under "None."

deputy commissars added immediately after the war began in 1941; the latter, however, headed more specialized services—artillery, logistics, and communications.

Much has been said in the West about the lack of professional experience within the Soviet military command after the purge, but this conclusion needs to be heavily qualified. The leaders just discussed had had a great deal of experience, though little of it was relevant to modern methods of warfare. But the sixty military commanders immediately subordinate to the generation born before 1891 (and this included the two youngest of the deputy commissars) had had a very different preparation.

First, the educational level of those just below the top was much better than that of their superiors, and better on the average than that of those who had been purged (see table 5-2). Like the new civilian appointees, the post-purge military commanders had usually been educated as adults, but their education had come even later in life than it had for the civilians. Few had been educated in tsarist military colleges or even in the Soviet academies of the early 1920s; almost all the commanders of fronts (the most important fighting units) and armies in 1941 with higher military education had graduated from the Frunze Academy between the late 1920s and the mid-1930s. On the average the front commanders had graduated in 1928, the army commanders in 1933.

Second, the fighting experience of these officials could be quite substantial. Those who graduated from the Frunze Academy in the 1930s had not been workers or low-level civilian political officers who had been sent to study there in their twenties. Instead, they had already been military officers for ten to fifteen years when they went to the academy. Approximately 65 percent of the front and army commanders in the first months of the war had not only fought in World War I, but had served as noncommissioned officers in it; approximately half had risen as high as division commander before the purge. Nearly all the front commanders had fought in the Soviet-Finnish War of 1939–40 or in the battles with the Japanese in the Far East in the late 1930s, as had at least one-third of the army commanders.[2]

The great unknown is the background of most of the officers below the level of army commander. It is known for certain that 500 to 1,000 of the top commanders (and, no doubt, an equal number of their political officers) were swept away in the purge, but it is not known how deeply the purge cut into the middle-level commanders and staff officers. Western estimates range from 20 to 40 percent of all officers,[3] and even though the lower estimate may well be two or three times too high, the real problems with trained leadership in 1941 were probably at the middle levels. Those with education had been swept up to the higher posts, and their replacements may have left much to be desired.

Nevertheless, the differences in the biographical patterns of the civilian and military elites of 1941 make it difficult to avoid the conclu-

2. A file of biographies was constructed by examining the six volumes thus far published of the *Sovetskaia voennaia entsiklopediia* , the thirty volumes of the third edition of the *Bol'shaia sovetskaia entsiklopediia*, and biographies and obituaries in the military newspaper *Krasnaia zvezda* from 1956 to the present. These statistical generalizations, as well as the others in this chapter, are based on this file. The biographies are not always complete on details of a career, and therefore some of the generalizations must be approximate.

3. See John Erickson, *The Soviet High Command: A Military-Political History, 1918–1941* (London: Macmillan, 1962), pp. 505–06.

sion that Stalin was quite conscious of what he was doing in the Great Purge. He clearly wanted his own Soviet elite—one that was overwhelmingly worker and peasant in its social origins and one little tainted by the tsarist or even the revolutionary past. He also thought that engineering education was appropriate for a civilian administrative elite leading a country through rapid industrialization and that military experience—especially military experience against a major Western power—was appropriate for his top generals. Morbidly suspicious though he may have been, Stalin did not let his suspicions destroy those he thought he needed. Irrational as the purge may sometimes have been with its widening circle of denunciations, the difference in age between the new military and civilian elites—particularly because it meant the survival in the military of men who had had the experience of being noncommissioned officers during World War I—suggests that Stalin kept the purge under sufficient control to permit his establishing the new elite he wanted.

Naturally the officers who served as the top command in the early months of the war did not all last for the duration. A few were courtmartialed and shot, others were killed in battle, and still others were demoted in the hectic effort to find commanders who could stop the early German advance. Yet many of the front and army commanders of the early period retained high command posts until the end, and the new ones were selected almost exclusively from the same narrow generation. The front commanders of 1941 had been born in 1895 on the average, and those of April 1945 in 1896; the army commanders of 1941 had been born in 1896 on the average, and those of April 1945 in 1898. The educational level of the new army commanders was marginally higher (62 percent of those in command at the end of the war had had higher military education), but performance in battle rather than possession of a degree was the essential requirement for promotion. The highest commander of them all, Georgii K. Zhukov, had not attended a military academy.

The same generation also took over command of the war in Moscow. The older deputy commissars who had fought in the First Cavalry Army during the civil war were eased out into relatively insignificant jobs, and the former tsarist colonel who had been chief of staff became ill and was named to head the Higher Military Academy. The top dozen officers in Moscow at the end of the war were born in 1897 on

Table 5-3. *Average Year of Birth of Top Military Officials, 1946–62*[a]

Year	Minister and deputy ministers[b]	Commanders of military districts[c]
January 1946	1897 (6)	1897 (30)
January 1950	1898 (10)	1898 (25)
January 1955	1897 (10)	1898 (18)
January 1960	1900 (12)	1902 (18)
January 1962	1900 (12)	1903 (18)

Source: See table 5-1.

a. The figures in parentheses indicate the number of officials included in each group.

b. For reasons of comparability, the deputy ministers of the navy are not included in the figures for the first two years, but the minister of the navy is. (After the death of Stalin, the head of the navy became a deputy minister of defense.)

c. Soviet troops stationed in East Europe are organized into "groups." As these are essentially equivalent to military districts in their size and significance, the group commanders are counted in with the commanders of military districts.

the average and had the same biographical profile as the other top military men.

The Fall and Rise of the Wartime High Command

An extended discussion of the characteristics of the top Soviet commanders in World War II may seem out of place in a book devoted to generational change decades later. In reality, however, the war is crucial for an understanding of what happened at the highest levels of the Soviet military for years after it ended. Front and army commanders of World War II still dominated the chief military posts well into the 1960s, and their role in the war—especially the relationships they formed with one another and with the political officers who served with them—seemed the main factor in determining the degree of their later success.

If one simply examines the ages of the top military leaders in the postwar period, one gains the impression of almost complete stability until the latter part of the Khrushchev era (early 1960s)—and even then the change was minimal (see table 5-3). Indeed, the same names of commanders keep reappearing year after year.

But though the generation of leading military commanders that won the war continued to hold the top positions in the military for the next fifteen years (and beyond, in many cases), the fates of individual generals were more variable. In particular, the almost unchanging statistics for the 1946–55 period hide a drastic shifting of men in and out of the central posts. Except for the commander of the air force and several high naval officials (one of whom was a holdover from the pre-purge period),[4] Stalin seems to have arrested none of his leading generals and admirals after the war. He did, however, banish almost all the most prominent ones from the center of policymaking.

The demotions began in 1946 with the biggest names of all. Early in that year Marshal Zhukov's name began disappearing from discussions about the war; in June he was sent to command the Odessa military district and later the Urals military district, both relatively insignificant ones. The minister of the navy, Nikolai G. Kuznetsov, was demoted to head of the educational institutions administration of the ministry; the commander of the air force, before being arrested, became head of a college preparing Aeroflot pilots; the deputy head of the general staff and the first deputy commander of the air force were named deputy commander of a military district and commander of an air army, respectively; and in 1948 the officer who had been the chief of staff at the end of the war became deputy commander of a military district. By 1951 two more deputy ministers of defense, the commander of artillery, and the first deputy minister of the navy were moved into marginal jobs.

Those who were commanders of the major fronts at the end of the war did a little better. None was demoted below the level of commander of military district, and this was in fact the post most of them occupied through the late Stalin period. In general, they commanded militarily important military districts or groups of troops abroad, but they were not given the posts that were the most politically sensitive. The Leningrad and Kiev military districts, as well as the troops in Germany, were headed by men who had risen only to the level of army commander in the war, and the Moscow military district was commanded by a former NKVD (secret police) general with no fighting experience in the war. For four years the infantry was headed by a famous corps commander,

4. The Soviet generals who were captured by the Germans were usually sent to camps upon their return home, and one of the disgraced deputy commissars of 1941 from the First Cavalry Army was shot.

Ivan Konev, a rival of Zhukov's, until he too was sent to a relatively minor military district.

The only important World War II military figure to thrive in the late Stalin period was Alexander M. Vasilevsky, Zhukov's chief of staff in Moscow throughout most of the period. He served as Nikolai Bulganin's first deputy minister from 1946 to 1949 and then became minister until Stalin's death. (From 1949 to 1950 he headed all the armed forces, but after the onset of the Korean War, the naval ministry was reestablished and Kuznetsov was brought back to head it.)

In the support and technical services, Vasilevsky's top deputies at the end of the Stalin period tended to be the deputies to the wartime leaders in their respective areas, but the posts more central to leadership of combat troops were usually assigned to officers without high-level, distinguished command experience. The first deputy minister, Vasilii D. Sokolovsky, had spent most of the war as chief of staff at a number of fronts, most notably Zhukov's fronts, and many other high officials were drawn from among former staff officials. The heads of the navy from 1947 to 1951 and of the air force throughout the postwar period had spent the entire war in the Far East. The one long-term front commander among the deputy ministers had been in charge of the relatively static Leningrad front from 1942 to 1945. Stalin gave the impression of a man who thought he might need his top World War II commanders because of the cold war (as he decided he did need Kuznetsov during the Korean War) but who was taking as few chances as possible of becoming the victim of a military coup.

Paradoxically, the civilian political leaders who had been most deeply involved in military operations during the war apparently did not arouse the same suspicions, for they prospered. Bulganin, a former mayor of Moscow and the top political officer on central fronts defending Moscow before he became deputy minister of defense in 1944, was promoted to minister in 1946 and then to deputy chairman of the Council of Ministers in 1949. He was named a member of the Politburo and served as Stalin's chief lieutenant for supervising the military and the defense industries. (Voroshilov, the old civil war hero, was also a deputy chairman of the Council of Ministers, but he was now responsible for coordinating the work of education, culture, and science.[5])

5. V.S. Akshinsky, *Kliment Efremovich Voroshilov*, 2d ed. (Moscow: Politizdat, 1976), p. 235.

Similarly, Andrei F. Zhdanov, the first secretary in Leningrad, who served as the top political officer on the fronts in that area during the war, became Stalin's chief lieutenant in the Central Committee Secretariat and really the number-two man in the political system until his death in 1948. The following year, Nikita Khrushchev, the Ukrainian first secretary who had been the top political officer on a number of fronts (including Stalingrad) before the Ukraine was liberated (and who had fought in the First Cavalry Army during the civil war), was moved to Moscow as the Central Committee secretary for supervision of the lower party apparatus.

It was precisely the two surviving political leaders who had been at the front during World War II who moved to the fore after Stalin's death. Khrushchev became leader of the Central Committee Secretariat almost immediately, and Bulganin was named first deputy chairman of the Council of Ministers and minister of defense. Over the succeeding months, Khrushchev was able to strengthen his position steadily, and by early 1955 was able to remove his principal rival, Georgii Malenkov, from the chairmanship of the Council of Ministers. Bulganin was the man chosen to replace him.

With the rise of Khrushchev and Bulganin the leading wartime commanders returned to Moscow. Zhukov was appointed Bulganin's first deputy minister of defense immediately after Stalin's death and replaced Bulganin as minister when the latter was promoted. Zhukov retained his close wartime associates Sokolovsky and Vasilevsky as first deputy ministers, and Aleksei I. Antonov, the chief of staff at the end of the war, returned as first deputy chief of staff, the post he had held under Vasilevsky throughout most of the war. Over the next three years, five wartime front commanders—Ivan Bagramian, Ivan Konev, Rodion Malinovsky, Kirill Meretskov, and Konstantin Rokossovsky—became deputy ministers (in one case, assistant minister) of defense, a sixth became first deputy commander of the infantry, and a seventh the head of the inspector-general corps. The key scientist in the wartime development of radar was appointed deputy minister of defense, undoubtedly for questions related to technological innovation.[6]

6. This man, A.I. Berg, was not identified as a deputy minister in the press at the time, nor was his successor, A.V. Gerasimov. However, the biographies of both men, with this post included, were printed in the *Sovetskaia voennaia entsiklopediia* (Moscow: Voenizdat, 1976–78), vol. 1, p. 44, and vol. 2, p. 525. Gerasimov was specifically identified as the deputy minister for radio-electronics, and this was probably Berg's title as well.

This reassembling of the wartime command meant, of course, that there would be a significant age difference between the top military and the top civilian officials. The civilian ministers averaged fifty-two years of age in early 1957; the minister of defense was sixty-one and his deputy ministers fifty-nine. Even at the next level of command within the ministry in Moscow—the thirty top subordinates of the deputy ministers[7]—the average age was not much lower—fifty-six. At the regional level, the party first secretaries were forty-eight years old, as against fifty-eight for the commanders and deputy commanders of the military districts.[8]

The Military and the Political Leadership

The relationship of the military to the party has fascinated Western scholars, and Stalin's actions suggest that he too paid great attention to the subject. This interest is scarcely surprising. In the twentieth century, developing countries—and the Soviet Union has been one throughout most of this period—have been particularly susceptible to military coups. Yet none has occurred in Communist countries.

In trying to explain the absence of military coups or even attempted coups in the Soviet Union, Westerners have largely focused upon the political structure that exists within the Ministry of Defense and is parallel to the regular chain of command. This political structure—and the names of its parts—changes from time to time, but at present there is a Main Political Administration at the summit, important political officers in the administrative subunits of the general staff, political administrations in the major forces (ground forces, navy, air force, air defense and, since 1959, strategic missiles), political administrations in military districts and fleets, and political departments in subdivisions down to the company level.

7. Strictly speaking, this should be "thirty of the top subordinates," but the biographical data are fairly complete for this year, and the thirty probably would be included in the top thirty-five or forty of the ministry.

8. Complete age information has been found on the commanders of military districts, but only twelve biographies of men who were deputy commanders, chiefs of staff, or assistant commanders—perhaps one-eighth of the total—are available. Their average year of birth was 1899, the same as for the commanders. It is not certain how representative this sample is, but the younger commanders of military districts of the 1960s, almost all of whose biographies are available, had rarely reached the level of deputy commander of military district by 1957.

Since the war the political officers in the military have nearly all been professional military men, but, especially in recent decades, they have been promoted almost exclusively within the military-political hierarchy, whereas the military commanders have been promoted within the regular command hierarchy. In civilian life a chairman of an executive committee of a provincial soviet is often promoted to the first secretaryship of the provincial party committee, and, in industry, an engineer is frequently a secretary of a plant primary party organization before going on to become plant manager. The head of a political administration of a military district, on the other hand, is never appointed commander of a district.

In Western studies the tendency has been to equate "political control of the Soviet armed forces" (the title of a recent book on the subject) with control by the political organs within the military or with the appointment of a civilian minister of defense.[9] Even in a book that emphasizes Khrushchev's close ties with the commanders who fought with him at Stalingrad, the Main Political Administration is still identified with the party and treated as its "central control organ in the military establishment."[10] There has also been a tendency to think that "the relationship between the Communist Party and the Soviet military is essentially conflict-prone and thus presents a perennial threat to the political stability of the Soviet state,"[11] and to see presumed rises and falls in the status of the Main Political Administration as a reflection of changes in the strength of party control.

But Timothy Colton has shown the importance of the Main Political Administration as a control instrument and the degree of conflict between the military commanders and the political officers have been much exaggerated.[12] The political officers are generally lower in rank than the commanders with whom they serve, and they are lower in other kinds of status, including status within the party. They are not simple watchdogs but have major administrative responsibilities in the supervision of indoctrination work among the troops, the military

9. Michael J. Deane, *Political Control of the Soviet Armed Forces* (New York: Crane, Russak, 1977). This book strongly exhibits the indicated tendency.

10. Roman Kolkowicz, *The Soviet Military and the Communist Party* (Princeton University Press, 1967), p. 358.

11. Ibid., p. 11.

12. Timothy J. Colton, *Commissars, Commanders, and Civilian Authority: The Structure of Soviet Military Politics* (Harvard University Press, 1979).

press, the network of clubs and cultural facilities for troops, and so forth. Because they take a special interest in the living conditions of the troops, they can become much involved in overseeing the supply system. In carrying out these responsibilities, the political officer finds it easy to fall into the role of an associate and even subordinate of the commander rather than of a rival or enemy.

In surveying memoirs both from the civil war and World War II, Colton found that, despite individual incidents of conflict, the basic relationship between the commander and the political officer of a fighting unit was one of cooperation and friendship. The principal conflicts took place when the commander of one unit and his political officer fought with another commander and his political officer or, even more frequently, with higher authorities. Although memoirs that cover the postwar period are not published, there is a passing reference in Oleg Penkovsky's papers to the relationship of his close friend, Marshal Sergei Varentsov, chief of missiles and artillery for the ground forces, and General Andrei Pozovny, head of the political administration of the air defense troops. "He used to be Varentsov's Deputy at the First Ukrainian Front. They are close friends."[13]

Paradoxically, such friendship between political officers and their commanders has readily been made use of by the political leaders in trying to control the military. Khrushchev, Bulganin, and Brezhnev were all political officers during the war, and when they rose to power they often chose as top officials in the Ministry of Defense men with whom they had fought during the war, men in whom they presumably had a special trust.

Of course, in many instances relationships among Soviet military commanders or between them and their political officers may not have been friendly. Moreover, since Soviet generals were frequently shifted as front conditions changed, they made many contacts. By arbitrarily looking for contact at a particular place or with a particular person, one may come up with a larger group of "close allies" than existed in reality.

Consider, for example, the case of Nikolai I. Krylov, the commander in chief of the strategic missile forces from 1963 until his death in 1972. In the first year of the war he was chief of staff of an army en-

13. Oleg Penkovskiy, *The Penkovskiy Papers*, trans. Peter Deriabin (Doubleday, 1965), p. 318.

gaged in the defense of Odessa and then Sevastopol, where, one would think, he had close contact with the commander of the Azov flotilla in that area, Sergei Gorshkov, an associate of Brezhnev and a future commander of the navy. In the second half of 1942 Krylov was chief of staff of Vasilii I. Chuikov's legendary Sixty-second Army, which held the center of the city of Stalingrad—an army directly under Khrushchev's supervision. During the battle of Kursk he was an army commander in a front headed by Sokolovsky; later his army was at a turning point in a battle that Vasilevsky was directing for the central headquarters.[14] Then in the postwar period Krylov served exclusively in the Far East, essentially as Rodion Malinovsky's first deputy. And none of this survey says anything about contacts and friendships he may have made in his prewar assignments and studies.[15]

It would be a mistake to state categorically that any one of these experiences was crucial to Krylov's future promotion, all the more so since he went through a number of promotions before reaching the final one. What probably happened was that he performed well in all the circumstances described and got favorably noticed by quite a few men who later were in a position to make the key decisions regarding him.

Nevertheless, there are groupings of generals who did fight together for long stretches of time; some of these groupings are closely associated with a party leader. For example, Bulganin had been the top political officer at three fronts near Moscow in the first three years of the war before he became deputy minister of defense in 1944 and Stalin's top deputy for military affairs in 1947. In 1955, when he was chairman of the Council of Ministers, the "highest level of the Soviet High Command" consisted of the minister of defense and four of his deputies— that is, Zhukov, Konev, Sokolovsky, Vasilevsky, and the air force commander, Pavel F. Zhigarev.[16] The first three had been commanders of fronts where Bulganin was the chief political officer, Vasilevsky

14. A. Kondratovich, *Rubezhi polkovodtsa* (Moscow: Politizdat, 1973), pp. 107-11.

15. For example, four World War II front commanders (Zhukov, Rokossovsky, Eremenko, and Bagramian) and at least two of the army commanders (P.L. Romanenko and V.I. Chistiakov) had been in the same study group admitted to the Higher Cavalry School in 1924. In his memoirs Bagramian describes how his friendship with Zhukov, which dates from that period, was instrumental in getting him the job he wanted on Zhukov's staff in 1940. I.Kh. Bagramian, *Tak nachinalas' voina* (Kiev: Dnipro, 1975), pp. 9-14.

16. Raymond L. Garthoff, "The High Command and General Staff," in B.H. Liddell Hart, ed., *The Red Army* (Harcourt, Brace, 1956), p. 255.

had been at central headquarters with him and had served as his first deputy in the postwar period, and Zhigarev (who had served the war in semidisgrace in the Far East)[17] was given the air force portfolio for the last four years of the Stalin period. Another general from the Moscow Front, Leonid A. Govorov, was the deputy minister in charge of the air defense forces until his death in 1955. Even though rumors suggested that Bulganin, as a political marshal, was hated by the professional generals, the composition of the top command at this time was not likely to have been a coincidence. Nor is it likely to have been a coincidence that within three years of Bulganin's involvement with the anti-party group in 1957 Zhukov and his four deputies were dismissed.

The most famous groupings of successful generals are those that can be linked in one way or another with Khrushchev during the war. In some cases the link may well have been coincidental, for it was almost inevitable that many top generals would have had contact with him at that time. After the important battles in 1941 around Leningrad and Moscow, the central German thrust had been in the southern part of the country where Khrushchev was party first secretary in the Ukraine. (Compare the 1942 May and November lines in the north and south in figure 5-1.) In the opening months of the war, Khrushchev served as the chief political officer of the Southwest Direction (*napravlenie*) that commanded the two fronts in the Ukraine. Then he became the chief political officer of one of the fronts that retreated to Stalingrad—the front that later supervised the final defense of the heart of the city. Subsequently he served in the same post on one of the fronts at the great battle at Kursk—the front that was positioned to liberate Kiev and did in fact do so. Moreover, as Konstantin Rokossovsky (a commander at a neighboring front both at Stalingrad and Kursk) reported, "As a member of the Politburo, [Khrushchev's] activity extended upon the boundaries of one front."[18] In particular, after he resumed the first secretaryship of the Ukraine following the liberation of Kiev, he of course remained vitally interested in the four fronts that were completing the expulsion of the Germans from the republic.

17. Zhigarev had been commander of the entire air force at the beginning of the war, but in 1942 had been sent to command the air force of the inactive Far East Front. In 1946 Bulganin brought him back as his first deputy commander of the air force, and in 1949 he became commander. *Sovetskaia voennaia entsiklopediia*, vol. 3, p. 334.

18. *Krasnaia zvezda*, August 4, 1963, p. 2. Nevertheless, Rokossovsky states that Khrushchev visited the staff of his front only a few times.

Given the scope of the military activity that took place as the Germans advanced and then retreated across the Ukraine, and given the fact that Stalingrad and Kursk were two of the three most important battles of the war (Moscow was the third), many of the generals who fought there would, in the natural course of events, be destined for important positions in the postwar period. Even so, the number of top military men of the Khrushchev era who had fought in the south was striking. Between 1956 and 1964, fifteen men were appointed deputy ministers of defense, and thirteen of them had fought in the south.[19] Indeed, the other two were not deputy ministers who supervised combat troops of any kind, one of them being the post-1963 deputy minister for construction and quartering of troops and the other the deputy minister for radioelectronics.[20]

The generals linked with Khrushchev have been called the Stalingrad group, but that name is rather misleading. Only seven fought at Stalingrad, and two of them were at Stalingrad fronts that competed with Khrushchev's.[21] The future party leader was the chief political officer with Andrei Eremenko, the commander of the original Stalingrad Front. As the situation grew worse, the front was split; Rokossovsky, one of the heroes of the Moscow battle, was sent in and given control of the larger half (the Don Front). Then a third front, the Southwest, was created out of the Don as part of the preparation for the great counteroffensive. Khrushchev had no role in coordinating the activities of the other fronts, for that function was given to headquarter representatives who had been sent in (notably Zhukov, Vasilevsky, and Malenkov). In December Eremenko (and Khrushchev) was deprived of the honor of finishing the defeat of Frederick Paulus's encircled army and was sent with a small group of armies in the direction of Rostov.[22]

19. Actually Ivan Bagramian was a deputy minister in 1954 and 1955, but was then appointed head of the Academy of the General Staff. He was reappointed deputy minister in 1958.

20. A.N. Komarovsky and A.V. Gerasimov.

21. Konstantin Rokossovsky and Vladimir Sudets. For hints of further rivalry when Khrushchev and Rokossovsky were on neighboring fronts during the Kursk battle, see K.K. Rokossovsky, *Soldatskii dolg* (Moscow: Voenizdat, 1968), pp. 224–25. For another study emphasizing a broad "southern group" instead of a Stalingrad one, see Raymond Garthoff, *Soviet Military Policy* (Praeger, 1966), pp. 46–56.

22. For a short description of the campaign and for excellent maps, see Earl F. Ziemke, *Stalingrad to Berlin: The German Defeat in the East* (Government Printing Office, 1968), pp. 16, 37–80. For Eremenko's (and one suspects—although he denies it—

Figure 5-1. *USSR Front Lines, May 1, 1942, and November 18, 1942*

Source: Earl F. Ziemke, *Stalingrad to Berlin: The German Defeat in the East* (Government Printing Office, 1968) p.16.

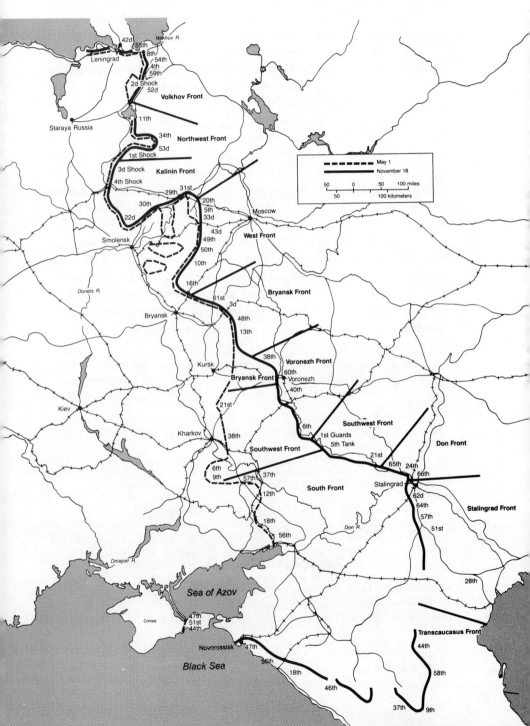

Khrushchev's thirteen deputy ministers really came from different battle areas. One group fought under the command of the Southwest Direction in the first six months of the war. (This direction, of which Khrushchev was the chief political officer, coordinated the activites of two fronts—the Southwest, which defended the northern half of the Ukraine and southern Russia, and the South, which defended the southern Ukraine.) One of the future deputy ministers had served in a high staff position in the direction, another fought throughout in the Southwest Front, and seven had been in the South Front.[23] Only three of the nine were in the armies that retreated toward Stalingrad; five others moved back toward Transcaucasia. A second group of three generals first fought in the south at Stalingrad and then joined Rodion Malinovsky's front, which then went on to liberate the Donbass.[24] A final general joined the war in the south in October 1943 as chief of staff of the Second Ukrainian Front, first under Konev and then under Malinovsky.[25]

At the end of the war, the high-prestige war theater was that aimed directly at Germany itself;[26] it comprised twenty-four Soviet armies, which were organized in three fronts under the direction of Zhukov, Konev, and Rokossovsky. The three southern fronts, which contained thirteen Soviet armies, had the responsibility of capturing Bulgaria, Rumania, Hungary, Czechoslovakia, and Yugoslavia. Despite the rel-

---

Khrushchev's) reaction to loss of the final Stalingrad victory, see G.K. Zhukov, *Vospominaniia i rasmyshleniia* (Moscow: Novosti, 1969), pp. 456–57, and Nikita Khrushchev, *Khrushchev Remembers*, trans. and ed. Strobe Talbott (Little, Brown, 1971), pp. 198–99.

23. The staff man was Ivan Bagramian, the Southwest Front general was Kirill Moskalenko, and the seven from the South Front were Sergei Gorshkov (actually an admiral in the Black Sea who fought with the front and under its supervision), Andrei Grechko, Nikolai Krylov, Rodion Malinovsky, Mitrofan Nedelin, Alexander Shebunin, and Konstantin Vershinin. (Nedelin was appointed deputy minister in 1955.) Moskalenko, Krylov, and Malinovsky were at Stalingrad. All the others except for Bagramian went to the Caucasus.

24. These were Sergei Biriuzov, Vasilii Chuikov, and Vladimir Sudets.

25. Matvei Zakharov.

26. See A.M. Vasilevsky, *Delo vsei zhizni* (Moscow: Politizdat, 1974), p. 532, and S.M. Shtemenko, *General'nyi shtab v gody voiny, Kniga vtoraia* (Moscow: Voenizdat, 1973), p. 371. For the acute disappointment of Moskalenko when he was taken out of one of the Germany fronts and of Rokossovsky when he lost the front that was aimed directly at Berlin, see K.S. Moskalenko, *Na iugo-zapadnom napravlenii, 1943–1945*, 2d ed. (Moscow: Nauka, 1973), vol. 2, pp. 490–92, and Seweryn Bialer, *Stalin and His Generals: Soviet Military Memoirs of World War II* (Pegasus, 1969), p. 615.

ative size and prestige of the three southern fronts, nine of the thirteen Khrushchev deputy ministers ended the war in this area, and a tenth was on a less prestigious front to the north of the Berlin Direction.[27]

The linchpin of the group among the generals was Malinovsky, who was to be named minister of defense in 1957. He had fought in the South Front (and for a time in the Southwest), commanding the South Front from December 1941 until July 1942, and had been at Stalingrad with Khrushchev. Khrushchev reported that at that time he had intervened with Stalin to defend Malinovsky from grave suspicions that had arisen about him.[28] Khrushchev clearly respected and trusted Malinovsky, who, along with the other men that had fought with Khrushchev, became his main instrument for controlling the military.[29]

Personnel selection is, however, a complicated matter. Often many people are consulted, and a number of opinions may go into the final decision. The story of the Khrushchev control of the military, let alone the post-Khrushchev control, would not be complete without including Leonid Brezhnev. Brezhnev, who rose in the Ukrainian party organization under Khrushchev both before and, especially, after the war, was brought to Moscow in 1952 as a Central Committee secretary— either the secretary for the police and the military or the secretary for heavy industry and the defense industry. Immediately after Stalin's death, Brezhnev was demoted to the post of deputy head of the Main Political Administration of the Armed Forces for a year, where he must have served as Khrushchev's eyes and ears. Then after two years in Kazakhstan supervising the introduction of the Virgin Lands program, Brezhnev returned as Central Committee secretary for heavy industry, the defense industry, and the space program. "In those years [his] office was a kind of staff where the most important problems of rocket construction were decided and where conferences were conducted with the most prominent scholars, designers, and specialists of different branches of science, technology, and production taking part."[30] In that capacity he also maintained a good deal of contact with the military.

27. Chuikov, Krylov, and Vershinin were in the Berlin Direction, Bagramian was to the north of it, and the others were to the south.

28. Khrushchev, *Khrushchev Remembers*, pp. 202–05.

29. See Nikita Khrushchev, *Khrushchev Remembers: The Last Testament* (Little, Brown, 1974), pp. 15–17.

30. V. Tolubko, *Nedelin: Pervyi glavkom strategicheskikh* (Moscow: Molodaia gvardiia), p.183.

Brezhnev too had been in the army throughout most of the war, as well as for a year afterward. Before the war, he had been secretary of the Dnepropetrovsk regional party committee for the defense industry; when Dnepropetrovsk fell, he first became deputy head of the political administration of the South Front and then head of the political department (the number-two political officer of the army, subordinate to the member of the military council) of the Eighteenth Army. This army spent the first two years of the war in the south, almost all of it in Caucasia. After the liberation of Kiev, the army was transferred to the front west of Kiev, then moved in a westerly direction for the rest of the war, eventually fighting in Czechoslovakia.

As a consequence, Brezhnev had had associations with many of the Khrushchev generals. He met Malinovsky in 1941 when the latter commanded the army that was defending Dnepropetrovsk; in 1942 Malinovsky commanded the South Front when Brezhnev was deputy head of its political administration. (Although Brezhnev was not there at the time, Malinovsky's front had also been the one to liberate Dnepropetrovsk.) Brezhnev must have had a close relationship with Andrei A. Grechko, for the latter once commanded the Eighteenth Army and throughout the war often commanded an army that adjoined the Eighteenth. Brezhnev's relationship with Admiral Sergei Gorshkov was probably close too, for the Eighteenth Army was stationed on the coast in late 1942 and most of 1943 and then took part in the amphibian attack that liberated Novorossisk (the famous *Malia zemlia* operation). Gorshkov at the time was deputy commander of the Novorossisk defense zone in charge of the naval forces.[31] The future general secretary may also have had contact with Mikhail A. Suslov, who was head of the partisans in Stavropol territory in the Caucasus.[32]

After fighting in the Caucasia-Transcaucasia theater from which five deputy ministers came, Brezhnev's Eighteenth Army was sent to the

31. *Krasnaia zvezda*, April 28, 1976, p. 2. When one of the foremost marshals dies, *Krasnaia zvezda* prints not only a standard obituary but also a personal tribute by one of the deceased's closest friends and associates. When Grechko died, Gorshkov was the man chosen for this task, and he emphasized how closely he had come to know Grechko in the battles around Novorossisk.

32. Considering the vast amount of memoir literature that has been published on the military and the partisans during the war, it is astonishing how little has been written about Suslov's role in the partisans. (He himself has apparently written no memoirs on the subject.) That which I have seen suggests conflict with the local military rather than cooperation. A.A. Grechko, *Bitva za Kavkaz*, 2d ed. (Moscow: Voenizdat, 1971), pp. 198, 277.

Ukraine, where it fought the last year and a half of the war in close proximity not only to Grechko's First Guard Army, but also to Kirill Moskalenko's Thirty-eighth Army. (The relative position of the three armies was switched occasionally, but essentially they tended to move as a phalanx.) The member of the military council for Moskalenko's army during this period, it should be noted, was Aleksei Epishev, the man who was named to head the Main Political Administration of the Armed Forces in 1962 and who has held that post since.[33] In the last months of the war Brezhnev was promoted to be head of the political administration of the Fourth Ukrainian Front (again, the number-two spot among the political officers), and, as such, he was supervising political work in both Grechko's and Moskalenko-Epishev's armies.

The large number of the Khrushchev generals who were linked with Brezhnev can surely be in part attributed to his advice and to the key role he played in the Khrushchev regime, especially with regard to the military. When Brezhnev himself became general secretary, he used his personal friendships with these wartime colleagues to consolidate his own control over the military. Upon Malinovsky's death in 1967, Grechko was appointed minister of defense and retained that post until his death in 1976; he was even given a full membership on the Politburo in his last years. (Grechko was replaced by a former defense industry administrator, Dmitrii F. Ustinov, who obviously had had a great deal of contact with the former Central Committee secretary for the defense industry and whom Brezhnev indeed referred to in public in the familiar form of "you"—"*ty.*"[34]) During the Brezhnev regime, Epishev remained the head of the Main Political Administration, Gorshkov the head of the navy, Moskalenko the head of the Ministry of Defense's chief inspectorate, and Peter Ivashutin (another general from the Caucasia-Transcaucasia theater) the head of military intelligence.

Generational Change

Obviously from what has just been said, the degree of generational change in the most sensitive control posts in the military has been minimal. In early 1980 Ustinov was seventy-one, Epishev seventy-one, Moskalenko seventy-one, Ivashutin seventy, and Gorshkov sixty-nine.

33. For Moskalenko's relationship with Epishev, see Moskalenko, *Na iugo-zapadnom napravlenii*, vol. 2, pp. 412–13.

34. *Pravda*, November 2, 1978, p. 1.

Table 5-4. *Average Age of Top Military Officials, 1950–80*[a]

Officials	January 1950	January 1960	January 1964	January 1967	January 1971	January 1980
First deputy ministers of defense	52	60	60	66	63	63
	(1)	(3)	(2)	(2)	(3)	(3)
Other deputy ministers of defense	51[b]	59	61	63	62	64
	(7)	(8)	(9)	(9)	(10)	(11)
Other top ministerial officials	49	56	58	59	58	61
	(18)	(40)	(40)	(41)	(42)	(30)
Commanders, military districts[c]	51	57	58	58	53	55
	(24)	(18)	(18)	(18)	(18)	(17)
Heads of political administration, military districts[d]	46[e]	51	54	55	53	55[f]
	(20)	(15)	(13)	(12)	(10)	(10)
First deputy commanders, military districts	n.a.	53	48	50	51	54
		(7)	(7)	(7)	(10)	(5)

Sources: See table 5–1.

n.a. Not available.

a. The figures in parentheses indicate the number of officials included in each group.

b. Includes the minister of navy.

c. Includes the commanders of the four groups of troops in East Europe.

d. Since 1957 these officials also bear the title of "member of the military district."

e. Members of military districts, who at this time were the superiors of heads of political administration. Because the exact date of service in the Stalin period is usually not available for political officers, the ones considered here served anytime in the period 1946–53.

f. Excludes one long-time friend of Brezhnev's who was born in 1906. The actual figure may be a year less because the officers for whom data are unavailable are newer and presumably younger.

Below this group, however, generational change has taken place during the Brezhnev era (see table 5–4).

In his memoirs Khrushchev reported, and agreed with, a statement by Zhukov that new commanders of military districts should be no older than fifty to fifty-five, but the men appointed to this post for the first time in the period 1960–64 were close to the upper limit of this range. By the time of Khrushchev's removal in late 1964, the average age of the commanders of military districts had risen to fifty-eight and that of the deputy ministers of defense to sixty-two. (The regional first secretaries, it may be remembered, were fifty-one, and the members of the Council of Ministers fifty-six.)

It was below the level of the commander of the military district that substantial change seems to have taken place in the late Khrushchev era. A relatively small sample of twelve first deputy commanders of military districts in the 1957–59 period were born on the average in 1904 (compared with 1901 for the commanders), but a sample of those

Table 5-5. *Age Distribution of Commanders and Deputy Commanders of Military Districts, 1948–80*

Period of birth	Commanders	Deputy commanders[a]
1890–94	8	1
1895–99	26	10
1900–04	27	11
1905–09	7	5
1910–14	11	8
1915–19	15	6
1920–24	19	21
After 1925	5	6

Sources: See table 5-1. Data on birth dates are also found in the regional press. The data on commanders are almost complete, the only missing men being four or five in the bottom two categories; the data on deputy commanders are based on a smaller sample.

a. Excludes deputy commanders who became commanders. In recent years the commanders of military districts have largely been selected from among deputy commanders, and their inclusion would increase the difference between the number of deputy commanders born in the period 1905–14 and those born later.

first deputy commanders serving in the 1961–64 period were born on the average in 1912 (compared with 1904 for the commanders). A group of lower military officials elected deputies to republican and regional soviets in 1963 were born on the average in 1915.

The reason for so little rejuvenation among the commanders of military districts in the Khrushchev period in comparison with lower categories is unclear, but the available biographical data suggest the existence of a generational gap—essentially of those officers born between 1905 and 1917 (see table 5-5). One possible explanation is that the division and corps commanders in World War II seem not to have been much younger than the army commanders. Consequently, the command experience during the war of those born between 1905 and 1917 was not much more extensive than that of those born between 1918 and 1923, and the leadership may have stayed with the more experienced older generation until a time when it was logical to switch to a much younger one. A second possible explanation is that the officers born between 1905 and 1917 may have had high mortality rates in the war. Not only were many lost in the disastrous encirclements of the early part of the conflict, but in the beginning lower-level officers were ordered to lead their troops into battle personally and thus were often among the first to be killed.

Whatever the reason, when generational change finally did occur in the military districts, it was a quite drastic one. The replacements for the military district commanders of January 1967 were on the average ten years younger than their predecessors. The process of replacement began in earnest after Malinovsky's death in March 1967, and though it took place over a number of years, it resulted in a decline in the average age of commanders from fifty-eight in 1967 to fifty-three in 1971. That means that in this short period the average year of birth went from 1908 to 1917. Although the generational change was not as sudden among the deputy ministers of defense, it was rather thorough at this level too. In 1967 their average year of birth was 1903; by the end of 1972 it was 1912.

In the 1970s the average age of the leading military officials gradually rose again. In early 1980, at fifty-five years of age, the commanders of the military districts remained younger than their counterparts at the end of the Khrushchev era, but the heads of the major fighting services—the army, the navy, and the air force—were sixty-eight and their first deputies were sixty-three. The youngest group of top officers in Moscow were in the general staff, where the chief of staff was sixty-two, and his three first deputies averaged fifty-seven.

With the exception of a few commanders of fleets in the navy, one almost never finds members of the postwar generation among the heads of administrations in the Ministry of Defense, the deputy commanders of the branch services, or the commanders of military districts or fleets. Only two men born as late as 1926 have been identified among the commanders and only three such men among sixty recent deputy commanders of military districts whose ages are known. At this level the only post where many new appointments have come from the postwar generation is that of head of the political administration of the military districts, although conceivably the new deputy commanders of the fleets may be increasingly coming from this group.

The reason that the postwar generation has not begun making a breakthrough in the military as it has in the civilian sector must be the same reason that led Stalin not to purge all the officers who had had lower command experience in World War I: a reluctance on the part of the leadership to move to a generation that has had no experience with war. In his memoirs Andrei Grechko recalled his first battle, and since he had just graduated from the elite Soviet military institute (the Academy of the General Staff), it seems certain that this experience had a great impact on his attitude toward personnel policy for years to come:

> In the first battle [my] 34th cavalry division was placed within the 5th cavalry corps. I tried to organize the combat in accordance with all the rules of academic science, in close correspondence with those 'ideal' injunctions which we diligently studied in the academies. . . . But it turned out that we did not have the practical skills of conducting reconnaissance, of organizing interactions and stable communication, and much else that war demanded. And the problem, of course, was not that we were poorly taught, but that it was much more difficult than we supposed to apply theory in battle conditions against a strong and more experienced enemy.[35]

Other officers were undoubtedly affected in the same way.

Obviously, at some level in the military command, the key posts are occupied by officers with no practical experience of large-scale war. The location of this breaking point is unclear, because the Soviet Union publishes almost no information on personnel below the level of deputy commander of military district. Even the age data on officers who are deputies to soviets are not terribly useful for this purpose, for the post of the officer is usually not given and many are political officers, who tend to be younger. At present most members of the wartime generation are still in their fifties, so there is no evident reason to retire them. Within a few years, however, a real choice will have to be made between age and experience, and it will be interesting to see how the Soviet Union handles this dilemma.

Changes in Values

The fact that Westerners have had less contact with the military in the Soviet Union than with any other of that country's specialized elites makes it especially difficult to analyze any evolution of the views within the military. Nevertheless, the available evidence suggests that Soviet officers have undergone considerable evolution in their professional attitudes.

The army itself has certainly changed. In 1939 only 12 percent of all officers and soldiers had completed secondary education or better, but this figure rose to 46 percent in 1964 and 80 percent in 1978. The number of different specialties in the military rose from 15 or 20 in World

35. A.A. Grechko, *Gody voiny, 1941–1943* (Moscow: Voenizdat, 1976), p. 7.

War I to 160 in World War II to 400 in the early 1950s to almost 2,000 in the late 1970s.[36] In World War II technology was very scarce and expensive, whereas manpower was unskilled and plentiful; Soviet military tactics reflected that fact. Now that technology is more plentiful and that the soldiers who operate it require much more training, officers have had to develop a careful attitude about the use of manpower.

The officers themselves also seem to have changed along with the army. In 1978 one-half of all officers had higher military and specialized military education, two and one-half times the level that had existed just a decade before.[37] Ninety percent of regiment commanders now have higher military education, and almost 100 percent of commanders of brigades and higher.[38] Changes in attitude are more difficult to document, but articles today do talk about the "culture" and the "intellectuality" of the officer.[39] Khrushchev reported in his memoirs that during World War II superiors might strike a subordinate officer when displeased with his performance.[40] Today the head of a faculty of the Academy of the General Staff may feel it necessary to complain about a tendency for officers to phrase commands as requests rather than in imperative language.[41] The articles of the commanders themselves show increased absorption with questions of management, the difficulties of coordinating the activities of so many technically trained subordinates, and the best techniques of educating and training the troops.

The evidence on possible change in the military officers' relationship to the rest of society and the outside world is almost nonexistent. In the Soviet Union, as elsewhere, the military tends to be a profession rather isolated from civilian society. Although the Soviet regime tries to keep leading officers familiar with civilian problems by having them elected to the soviets and leading party committees (13,351 were elected deputies to the local soviets in 1974),[42] its preoccupation with military secrecy must work in the other direction. Furthermore, there seems to be some tendency for the military to be drawing into itself.

36. *Krasnaia zvezda*, January 12, 1978, p. 3; December 9, 1976, p. 2.
37. Ibid, January 7, 1978, p. 2.
38. Ibid., June 3, 1976, p. 3.
39. Ibid., March 11, 1972, p. 2.
40. *Khrushchev Remembers*, p. 170.
41. *Krasnaia zvezda*, January 21, 1977, p. 2.
42. Ibid., May 16, 1974, p. 3.

Surveys of students in military institutes show a large proportion coming from military homes (in one poll, 30 percent cited "family tradition" as the reason for enrolling),[43] and a number of commanders of military districts are sons of World War II generals.[44] The reading habits of the military also seem insular. A survey of 1,000 young lieutenants found that 55 percent subscribed to the military newspaper *Krasnaia zvezda* and 28 percent to the newspaper of the military district, as against 39 percent to *Pravda* and 16 percent to *Izvestiia*.[45]

What this means about the attitudes of the military is difficult to say. Professionals usually believe in the worth of their profession and tend to develop ideologies that support its goals. One would not expect the military in any country to convince itself of the non-threatening nature of the country's major adversary. *Krasnaia zvezda*'s image of the American system and foreign policy has, in fact, tended to be more hard-line than that of, say, the Academy of Sciences journals,[46] and many officers must have joined the army feeling like the officer who reported: "I hate imperialism . . . in whatever form it takes. . . . I am ready to struggle with it to full victory and therefore selected service in the army."[47]

Yet the real question is one of trends and policy implications. It is unlikely that the Soviet military today is any more suspicious of the West and any more hostile toward it then the older generations within the military. World War II memoirists, even those who have written in the last decade, often go out of their way to attribute the most sinister motives to the Allied governments for their delay in opening a second front in Europe. Indeed, the present top career officer in the military, Chief of Staff Nikolai Ogarkov, who participated in the first strategic arms limitation talks with the United States, is said by well-informed Soviet citizens to be the first politically sophisticated Soviet marshal.

From a policy point of view, two questions are crucial. First, what

43. Ibid., January 17, 1970, p. 3.
44. Colton, *Commissars, Commanders, and Civilian Authority*, pp. 268–70.
45. *Krasnaia zvezda*, April 5, 1969, p. 3.
46. It should not be thought that everything in *Krasnaia zvezda* reflects the views of the military. Sometimes very sophisticated outsiders try to bring a different viewpoint to the military. See, for example, the article on disarmament by the deputy head of a Central Committee department, G. Shakhnazarov, in *Krasnaia zvezda*, June 14, 1979, pp. 2–3. Some of the hard-line articles may also be not expressions of official views, but attempts to influence them.
47. Ibid., April 5, 1969, p. 3.

Table 5-6. *Fears about the Future among Students in Military Institutes*[a]

Percent

	Students				
Fear[a]	*First year*	*Second year*	*Third year*	*Fourth year*	*Fifth year*
Moscow Troop School (Uchilishche)					
Distance of place of service	22	18	12	6	n.a.
Climate of place of service	6	10	8	8	n.a.
Need to answer for subordinates	20	22	20	20	n.a.
Complexity of the technology	20	25	15	8	n.a.
Difficulties in living conditions	12	15	26	48	n.a.
Nothing	20	10	19	10	n.a.
Higher Naval College					
Distance of place of service	18	18	15	10	6
Climate of place of service	7	4	3	3	2
Need to answer for subordinates	10	12	12	12	12
Complexity of the technology	24	18	15	13	18
Difficulties in living conditions	6	16	25	37	42
Nothing	35	32	30	25	20

Source: *Krasnaia zvezda*, January 17, 1970, p. 3.

n.a. Not applicable.

a. In answer to question, "What difficulties in the future disturb you the most?"

domestic consequences does the military draw from its concern about the American challenge? Second, how much impact does the military have upon foreign policy?

In the past the military seems to have supported a strong emphasis on heavy industry and the defense industry; presumably its point of view has not changed. It has shown concern about the values inculcated into the young, and this has led it to favor a conservative cultural policy. Conceivably it remains one of the strong forces opposing any significant change in the Soviet Union.

Nevertheless, there may be changes taking place in the military's attitudes toward domestic policy. One should not forget that members of the military are at the same time consumers. An interesting poll of military students shows the rising concern of students about living conditions as they approach graduation (see table 5–6). It is unlikely that such concern disappears until the officers advance well up in the hierarchy.

The question of technological innovation is also becoming more and more important to the military. In the past, military strength meant steel and tanks, but now the development of new weapons is more crucial, and these may depend upon the innovative capacity of the economy and the scientific community. If the military became convinced that the future growth of the economy and especially technological innovation depended on economic reform, they might well be inclined to be sympathetic—especially if deep down they suspect that reform may improve the consumers' sector.

If one is talking about generational change in Soviet defense analysis rather than just within the military, then other possible changes need to be mentioned. Most changes will stem from the fact that the next general secretary is almost certain to be a man who did not fight alongside his top military adviser in World War II. Possibly he will select as military leader someone he knew as commander of a regional military district, but the deep "front-line friendship" of which Soviet memoirists often speak will not be there. Consequently, one of the major mechanisms of control from the past would then be absent, the leader's relationship with the military therefore more professional. Since the military in industrialized countries has proved not to be a direct threat to civilian authority (in contrast to non-Communist third world experience), it is improbable that the danger of a military coup will increase, barring critical regime problems in maintaining order in the street. But a leader less intimately and personally tied with the military establishment may well seek new mechanisms of control or at least coordination.

In particular, the next general secretary may well be tempted to create a post analogous to national security adviser and to appoint a civilian to it. In the past the weapon development program seems to have been the exclusive domain of the military, the defense industry, the design bureaus, and the foremost political leadership. This complex guarded its monopoly jealously. In one of the most famous moments in the SALT I negotiations, Ogarkov reproached the American negotiators for revealing Soviet military secrets to the civilian negotiators (including the Soviet ones). Today the civilians in the Academy of Sciences institutes may still be denied access to Soviet military secrets, but they are assiduous readers of the American strategic literature and

the CIA estimates of the Soviet military might. The Institute of the
USA and Canada is beginning to train its own graduate students spe-
cializing in these questions (including—scandalously—two women) so
that it will not even have to rely upon former military officers for its
analysis. If a generational change within the military is accompanied
by a gradual rise in the role of the civilian foreign policy establishment
in strategic questions, its impact will be doubly significant.

6

The Foreign Policy Establishment

WESTERN observers are quite aware of the advanced age of the top Politburo members and of the ensuing problems created for the coming leadership succession. Far fewer recognize that similar problems exist for the Soviet foreign policy elite and that a complete turnover of personnel must surely take place within its core over the next five years. These changes deserve careful consideration, for a gap of some fifteen years exists between the top foreign-policy makers and those most likely to succeed them, at least in posts that deal with the West.

The locus of influence and power is not easy to determine. A relatively obscure adviser may have a decisive impact upon events, whereas a man in a high post may be frozen out of the process by which decisions are really made. Nevertheless, a person in a top position does have access to the inner circle, and if his views had been found unacceptable, he could have been—and normally would have been—replaced by someone whose perspective was more congenial.

If one defines the inner circle of the foreign policy establishment by the nature of their responsibilities and the Politburo or Central Committee status accorded them, the following seem to have been the inner fifteen in early 1980: Leonid I. Brezhnev, party general secretary and chairman of the Presidium of the Supreme Soviet; Aleksei N. Kosygin, chairman of the Council of Ministers; Mikhail A. Suslov, second secretary of the Central Committee and top foreign policy assistant to Brezhnev among the Central Committee secretaries;[1] Andrei A. Gromyko, minister of foreign affairs; Iurii V. Andropov, chairman of the KGB (an institution that has the functions of the CIA as well as those

1. Westerners often treat Andrei Kirilenko as the second secretary, for he exercises the overall supervision of the economy and the party apparatus that have been associated with that de facto post in the past. But at recent party congresses, Suslov has been listed as the second man in the Secretariat—and, of course, alphabetical order can scarcely explain that position. See *XXV s"ezd Kommunisticheskoi partii Sovetskogo Soiuza [24 fevralia–5 marta 1976 goda]*, *Stenograficheskii otchet* (Moscow: Politizdat, 1976), vol. 2, p. 328.

of internal security); Dmitrii F. Ustinov, minister of defense; Boris N. Ponomarev, secretary of the central committee and head of the international department; Konstantin V. Rusakov, secretary of the Central Committee and head of the socialist countries department; Vasilii V. Kuznetsov, first deputy chairman of the Presidium of the Supreme Soviet; Ivan V. Arkhipov, deputy chairman of the Council of Ministers and chairman of the Council of Ministers' Foreign Economic Commission; Nikolai S. Patolichev, minister of foreign trade; Semen A. Skachkov, chairman of the State Committee for Foreign Economic Relations (despite its title, really the foreign aid agency); Nikolai M. Pegov, head of the foreign personnel department of the Central Committee;[2] Andrei M. Aleksandrov-Agentov, personal assistant to the general secretary (with special responsibility for relations with the United States); and Anatolii I. Blatov, personal assistant to the general secretary (with special responsibility for relations with Western and Eastern Europe). Except for the two personal assistants, all these men are full members of the Central Committee, and eight of them are full or candidate members of the Politburo.

As one examines the biographies of these top foreign-policy makers, several facts become obvious. The first is the similarity in their backgrounds. As table 6-1 indicates, ten were born between 1904 and 1909, and nine were in college during the First Five-Year Plan period, 1928–32. Typically for that period, nine graduated from engineering institutes, one from an industrial academy, one from an agricultural institute, and one from a secondary specialized educational institution (technicum) for transportation. At least nine came from a worker or peasant family, and nearly all took a big step up when they were sent to college in the 1920s and the early 1930s. (Eleven were between twenty-five and thirty-three years of age when they graduated from college.) Only three are not members of the Brezhnev generation; the others are classic members.

A second striking fact about the top Soviet foreign-policy makers is the length of time during which they have had an opportunity to work together—an extraordinarily long period when compared with American experience. Indeed, six of the most important officials have held

2. It is possible that Pegov is not a significant figure in policymaking and is concerned only with personnel selection. However, he is a Central Committee member and has been an ambassador since 1956.

Table 6-1. *The Core of the Foreign Policy Establishment, 1980*

Name	Date of birth	Date of college graduation
Aleksandrov-Agentov, Andrei M.	1918	1940
Andropov, Iurii V.	1914	1936[a]
Arkhipov, Ivan V.	1907	1932
Blatov, Anatolii I.	1914	1940
Brezhnev, Leonid I.	1906	1935
Gromyko, Andrei A.	1909	1934
Kosygin, Aleksei N.	1904	1935
Kuznetsov, Vasilii V.	1901	1926
Patolichev, Nikolai S.	1908	1937
Pegov, Nikolai M.	1905	1938
Ponomarev, Boris N.	1905	1926
Rusakov, Konstantin V.	1909	1930
Skachkov, Semen A.	1907	1930
Suslov, Mikhail A.	1902	1928
Ustinov, Dmitrii F.	1908	1934

Source: 1977 yearbook of the *Bol'shaia sovetskaia entsiklopediia*.
a. Andropov actually graduated from a technicum in this year. He never graduated from a university.

their present jobs for at least twenty years. Suslov, for example, has been a Central Committee secretary since 1947 and a leading foreign policy official since at least 1954, when he was named chairman of the Foreign Policy Committee of one of the houses of the Supreme Soviet.[3] Gromyko was appointed minister of foreign affairs in 1957, but before that had been first deputy minister from 1949 to 1957 (with a short interruption as ambassador to Great Britain), and head of the American desk of the ministry (then called a people's commissariat) as early as 1939 and ambassador to the United States in 1943. Ponomarev worked in the executive committee of the Comintern in 1936 and was then moved into party work upon its abolition. Essentially he was the number-two man in the international department of the Central Committee from 1944 until he became its head in 1955. Kuznetsov's job was newly created in 1977, but from 1955 to 1977 he had been first de-

3. Suslov attended some Cominform meetings in the Stalin period and may well have had responsibility for relations with Eastern Europe. But his speech at the Nineteenth Party Congress in 1952 suggested his responsibility only for education, science, culture, internal propaganda, and the like—that is, the slot handled by P.N. Demichev and now M.V. Zimianin in the Brezhnev period.

puty minister of foreign affairs. Since 1958 Patolichev and Skachkov have been minister of foreign trade and chairman of the State Committee for Foreign Economic Relations respectively.

Another three in the inner circle of foreign policy officials have served in their posts for a decade or longer. Aleksandrov-Agentov has been Brezhnev's personal assistant since the early 1960s; Rusakov essentially head of the socialist countries department since 1968;[4] and Andropov (who was Rusakov's predecessor from 1957 to 1967), chairman of the KGB since 1967.

Ustinov has been minister of defense for a much shorter time (since Grechko's death in 1976), but from 1965 to 1976 had been Central Committee secretary in charge of the defense industry and the military and intimately involved in decisionmaking as a candidate member of the Politburo. (He had also been a USSR minister or higher in the defense industry from 1941 to 1965.) Arkhipov's tenure as deputy chairman of the Council of Ministers has likewise been limited to the period since 1974, but for the previous fifteen years he had been first deputy chairman of the State Committee for Foreign Economic Relations. He was one of the dozen or so men who had been a party official under Brezhnev's direct supervision in Dnepropetrovsk or Moldavia in the late 1930s and the 1940s and who had become prominent in the Brezhnev era. It is therefore quite likely that his real access to the inner circle of foreign-policy makers from 1959 to 1974 was greater than his governmental position would indicate. Only Pegov is a relative newcomer to the inner circle in Moscow, and even he became an ambassador in 1956, retaining his membership in the Central Committee.

It is incredible to think that in 1980 the head of the international department of the Central Committee (and a candidate member of the Politburo) had been appointed a key member of the Comintern executive committee to help implement the Popular Front in the 1930s, that the present minister of foreign affairs was serving as ambassador to the United States when Franklin D. Roosevelt was president, and that the principal Central Committee secretary for foreign policy was speaking before the Cominform at roughly the time of the Stalin-Tito split in

4. Rusakov actually holds two posts now—Central Committee secretary and department head—and the former post is a relatively new one. For a period he was Brezhnev's personal assistant for relations with socialist countries instead of Central Committee department head, but the latter position was left empty during that time.

1948. In no other major country have the same foreign policy officials been occupying such central posts for so long.

Yet precisely because of the age and tenure of these officials, it seems nearly certain that within five years—and probably much sooner—almost none of them will be having an impact on Soviet foreign policy. Even the three "younger" men—the KGB chairman, Andropov, and Brezhnev's personal assistants Aleksandrov-Agentov and Blatov—hold positions whose occupants have fared poorly in other periods of leadership transition. With a change in top foreign-policy makers imminent, the question that obviously interests everyone the most is what their successors will be like.

The Older Generation

Two-thirds of the top fifteen foreign-policy makers had first been appointed to posts in this area after Stalin's death, perhaps in part because of the peculiar impact of the purge on the foreign policy establishment. Despite the frequent assumption in the West that contact with foreigners made an official especially vulnerable to the Great Purge of 1937–38, a fairly high proportion of the leading foreign-policy makers actually survived it. Viacheslav Molotov, the top Politburo specialist on foreign policy was not touched, nor was the top Politburo specialist on foreign trade (Anastas Mikoyan), the Central Committee secretary who dealt with foreign affairs (Andrei Zhdanov), the commissar of foreign affairs (Maxim Litvinov), the chairman and secretary of the Comintern (Georgii Dimitrov and Dmitrii Manuilsky), the chairman of the Trade Union International (Solomon Lozovsky), or the director of the principal foreign policy research institute (Eugene Varga). The ambassadors to the United States, England, France, Italy, and Germany were also not arrested, although ambassadors to other countries often were.[5] On the eve of the war, the commissar of foreign affairs was Molotov (born in 1890); the first deputy commissar was Andrei Vyshinsky (born in 1883), a former Menshevik who had been the chief prosecutor in the show trials of 1936-38; and the three deputy

5. For a list of top officials purged, see Teddy J. Uldricks, "The Impact of the Great Purges on the People's Commissariat of Foreign Affairs," *Slavic Review*, vol. 36 (June 1977), pp. 188–89.

commissars were Litvinov (born in 1876), Lozovsky (born in 1878), and Vladimir Dekanozov (born in 1898). The situation was quite unlike that in commissariats dealing with internal policy, where the purge had eliminated most of the older men.

At levels below the top in the foreign policy establishment, the situation was also unlike that in other policy areas, but in the opposite way. In the party apparatus, in economic management, in the soviets, and in the military, the Great Purge brought incredibly quick promotion to the kinds of people who were in any case likely to receive it at a more leisurely pace over the next ten to fifteen years. The new officials tended to have received appropriate education in the late 1920s or the 1930s and to have worked in lower-level jobs in their specialty before being thrust upward.

Nothing of the sort happened in the foreign policy realm. Perhaps the problem was a lack of young men with the appropriate education to promote. Soviet social science education in the 1920s and the first half of the 1930s tended to be general in content, emphasizing broad class conflict rather than specific information. During the cultural revolution, the social science faculties were closed down altogether, and when they were reopened, the regime was emphasizing the importance of traditional history, with dates, leaders, concrete events, and so forth. Therefore, in the late 1930s, men with social science backgrounds who were in their late twenties and early thirties had received a type of training that the leadership had now repudiated. Perhaps younger men who had worked in the Commissariat of Foreign Affairs had also spent too much time abroad and, unlike older men, were thought to have been affected by foreign influences at an impressionable age.

Whatever the cause, almost no men in the foreign policy establishment who were in their thirties were promoted in the wake of the purge. Or at least if any such were promoted, almost none remained in their posts for long. (Diplomatic sources at the time reported that the really sweeping wave of removals of junior and middle-level officials of the Commissariat of Foreign Affairs occurred not in 1937–38, but in the spring of 1939, after Molotov replaced Litvinov as the commissar of foreign affairs.[6]) A Soviet biographical directory of scholars studying

6. *Foreign Relations of the United States: The Soviet Union, 1933–1939* (Government Printing Office, 1952), p. 772.

the Orient reveals a few commissariat officials of the 1930s who continued to work within it in the 1940s,[7] but almost none reached the rank of counselor, minister, or ambassador in the post-purge period. Except for the type of older, high-level officials already mentioned, only two of several hundred post-purge officials of this rank stationed either in Moscow or abroad had entered the diplomatic corps before 1936.[8]

The basic structure of the Commissariat of Foreign Affairs was (and is) geographical, and the basic officials below the level of deputy commissar were the heads of departments (*otdels*). Biographies have been found of thirteen men who held the post of departmental head in the period 1939–41. They were born in 1905 on the average (in fact, eight were born between 1904 and 1906). Their previous backgrounds varied, but they often had engaged in some kind of research or educational activity and a number had the Soviet equivalent of the Ph.D. degree. Their work invariably focused on the internal Soviet situation rather than on the outside world. Some of them graduated from the Institute of Diplomatic and Consular Officials, which had a short term of study, but most seem to have been appointed directly from the outside.

In short, the pattern of selection suggests that the regime was looking for officials who were relatively uncorrupted by foreign contact, but whose work had forced them to learn a foreign language and had demonstrated their ability to learn and communicate.[9] Although many had been sent abroad as part of some delegation or exchange, the biographical data indicate that many, if not most, of the department heads were administering a department that dealt with a part of the world they had never seen. Lower officials often had no foreign language.

A typical example of a new department head, though somewhat younger than the average, was Andrei Gromyko, who was appointed head of the American department in 1939. Gromyko, who was born in 1909, had joined the party in 1931, and until 1936 had been first a stu-

7. S.D. Miliband, *Biobibliograficheskii slovar' sovetskikh vostokovedov* (Moscow: Nauka, 1975). See, for example, the biographies of I.V. Samylovsky and A.F. Sultanov on pp. 494 and 537.

8. The biographies have been published in three editions of *Diplomaticheskii slovar'* (Moscow: Izdatel'stvo politicheskoi literatury, 1948–50, 1960–64, and 1971–73).

9. For a different assessment of the language ability of the replacement generation as a whole, see Uldricks, "Impact of the Great Purges on the People's Commissariat of Foreign Affairs," pp. 195–96.

dent in agricultural economics in Belorussia. Upon receiving his degree, he had gone to work in the Institute of Economics of the Academy of Sciences in Moscow, and in 1939 he was the responsible secretary of the institute's journal, *Voprosy ekonomiki*. From this post he received a direct appointment as head of the American countries department of the commissariat. Soon he was sent to Washington as a counselor at the Soviet embassy, and in 1943—at the age of thirty-four—he became ambassador to the United States.

The passage of time both eased and intensified the Soviet problem with diplomatic personnel. On the one hand, the outsiders like Gromyko gradually became more expert in the performance of their duties, and those who had been appointed to lower posts in embassies abroad brought their first-hand experience of foreign countries with them when they returned to Moscow. Officials were usually rotated between the field and the home office every three or four years, but the level of experience of the leading officials continuously rose throughout the Stalin period, for they were all chosen from the same generation. In 1946 the average department head of the Ministry of Foreign Affairs had been born in 1907 and had entered diplomatic work in 1939; in 1952 the average department head had been born in 1907 and had entered diplomatic work in 1940. The deputy ministers of 1952 had been born a year earlier and had had two more years of diplomatic experience.

On the other hand, the rise of the Soviet Union to Great Power status, coupled with the gradual increase in the number of independent countries in the third world, required a steady increase of personnel in the diplomatic corps. As a result, the regime continued to recruit men (and only men) from other lines of work into the Ministry of Foreign Affairs in the postwar period. For many years the average age of entry stayed at about thirty-one.[10] But after the immediate post-purge period, most entered the Ministry of Foreign Affairs at fairly low levels, often received training at the Higher Diplomatic Academy, and spent years rising upward in orderly fashion.

In other parts of the foreign policy establishment the situation was

10. The figure of thirty-one is based on the biographies of 269 men who first entered diplomatic work from 1936 through 1952. Since 233 of these men entered in the period from 1936 through 1948, the generalization may well not apply to the 1949–52 period when the number of biographies available is still rather small.

Table 6-2. *Distribution of Soviet Scholars in Oriental Studies by Field of Study and Year of Birth, 1935-53*[a]

Year of birth	Politics, economics[b]	Ethnography, geography	History, languages, literature[b]
1894 and earlier	13	1	72
1895–1905	54	3	86
1906–12	24	7	68
1913–19	12	3	55

Source: Calculated from the biographies in S. D. Miliband, *Biobibliograficheskii slovar' sovetskikh vostokovedov* (Moscow: Nauka, 1975). This source seems quite complete, although scholars who did not publish are excluded.

a. Scholars who studied the civilizations in Central Asia, Transcaucasia, and other areas now within the Soviet Union are excluded.

b. A historian whose work, or a significant part of it, comes within a decade or two of the present is included under politics and economics.

even worse in the 1940s. Journalists covering the outside world seem to have been particularly affected by the purge. Although the biographies of a few Soviet Orientialists indicate that scholars were sometimes recruited to fill the gap,[11] many posts were simply not filled, so that "a kind of 'vacuum' " was created.[12] In 1945 the leading governmental newspaper, *Izvestiia*, did not have a single foreign correspondent, and the Tass office in New York City was headed by an American until January 1944.[13]

By the early 1950s, as discussed further below, the conditions within journalism were gradually being corrected, but those within the scholarly community were falling into worse disarray. During the 1920s and early 1930s, a quite substantial community of those studying the outside world had been created, a large proportion of them in their thirties (those born between 1895 and 1905). These scholars were Marxists, unlike most of the traditional history and literature specialists and, no doubt, were of varying degrees of sophistication. The existence of the Comintern, however, at least gave them contact with the outside world and some sense of the international turmoil in left-wing politics.

Then a series of disasters befell Soviet social science. One can clearly see from table 6-2 the deteriorating situation in Oriental studies, which must be similar to that in European studies: in the late 1930s,

11. For example, see the biography of M.A. Korostovtsev in Miliband, *Biobibliograficheskii slovar' sovetskikh vostokovedov*, p. 273.

12. *Zhurnalist*, March 1967, pp. 16–17.

13. Ibid., June 1974, p. 71.

1940s, and early 1950s the proportion of "younger" scholars (those born after 1906) in the field of economics and politics was much lower than that proportion of scholars in the previous generation. Some scholars of the contemporary scene were hit by the purge,[14] and at roughly the same time a number of party institutes that had served as the base for many such scholars were closed. Contact with foreigners soon dried up. Except for Eugene Varga's Institute of the World Economy and World Politics and a new Pacific Institute opened during the war (incorporated into the Institute of Oriental Studies in 1950), the major remaining institutes for training young scholars were the traditional centers for the study of history or literature, supplemented by the Institutes of Geography and Ethnography. These centers, together with the colleges and universities (which did not teach contemporary politics and economics of foreign countries), provided the only jobs and so further shaped career choices. The war sharply curtailed all higher and postgraduate education, and in 1949 Varga's institute was closed after a hail of criticism directed toward scholars who overestimated capitalism's ability to survive. All these developments sharply reduced the number of people who studied the outside world and led to a retreat from politically dangerous contemporary subjects to much safer—and less policy-relevant—ones.

The Creation of a New Corps of Specialists

Since the shortage of trained young personnel was partly the result of the disruption of education during the war, the end of the war brought some relief for the problem. By the late 1940s and early 1950s the universities were once more turning out undergraduates and gradu-

14. Of the forty-seven specialists on the politics and economics of Asia and Africa who were born between 1895 and 1905 and who had entered scholarly work before the purge, 28 percent died in the period 1939–42 or apparently were sent to a concentration camp. Of the seventy-four specialists on history, languages, and literature of a like background, 20 percent died or disappeared in this period, but one-third of this group seem to have died of bombing or hunger in the Leningrad blockade. (Leningrad was the center for historical and literary work, whereas those working on politics or economics tended to be in Moscow.) These figures are calculated from the biographies in Miliband, *Biobibliograficheskii slovar' sovetskikh vostokovedov*. This source does not give the cause of death, and both figures are probably several percentage points high because a few of the deaths must have been natural.

ate students trained in history, some of whom made their way into the international field. In addition, three institutes began training undergraduates directly for this field. The old Moscow Institute of Eastern Studies seems to have added a substantial social science component to its undergraduate curriculum, and the Ministry of Foreign Trade's Institute of Foreign Trade seems to have expanded its enrollment. More important, an entirely new undergraduate institute was created in 1944: the Moscow State Institute of International Relations (MGIMO). Its first class graduated in 1948, and its second class—the legendary class of 1949—produced an unusually high proportion of the top advisers of the Brezhnev period.

MGIMO was attached first to Moscow University and then to the Ministry of Foreign Affairs. Its leading professors were drawn from Moscow University and other relevant institutes in Moscow on a part-time basis, and Ministry of Foreign Affairs officials also served as part-time instructors. For example, Anatolii Dobrynin, the present ambassador to the United States, led a seminar in the late 1940s. Compared with Moscow University, MGIMO had excellent language instruction, oral as well as reading. Some 300 students were admitted each year and grouped by the language they were studying. Perhaps one-third to one-half were in the English group; smaller numbers were in German and French. Spanish was not added until much later.

The students of the late Stalin period were to be the new elite in the realm of international relations, but in contrast to the policy followed in creating the domestic and the military elites in the late 1920s and early 1930s, no effort was made to draw into international relations students of working class or peasant origin. Complete data are available on the social backgrounds of 198 scholars working on the economics, ethnography, geography, and politics of Asia and Africa who were born in the 1920s. (Incidentally, it may be recalled from table 6-2 that in the late Stalin period there had been only 46 such scholars born between 1906 and 1919.) Seventy-four percent of these scholars come from white-collar families, and all the evidence suggests a similar percentage in every part of the foreign policy establishment.

Although MGIMO was later to become a prestigious institute to which members of the elite strove to send their sons, the competition to enter it was not severe in the early years, perhaps because of the memories of 1937–38. At least one man has admitted that after returning from the army, he chose to enroll in MGIMO rather than in an engineering institute because he had forgotten his mathematics during the war.[15] Some of the students were delivered to classes in their fathers' limousines and some (perhaps the same ones) "thought that they should be sent to different countries as ambassadors immediately after receiving their diplomas."[16] But such students, according to those who described them, were not the successful ones. For instance, the former student who mentioned his chauffeured classmates dismissed them with a self-satisfied "Where are they now?"

The members of the future foreign policy elite were also somewhat different in age from their future counterparts in civilian spheres. As has been mentioned, study of the outside world did not require mathematics and science. And the war may have helped to develop language skills among some in the military and a curiosity about the outside world in many others. Therefore, a substantial number of the wartime generation are found among the early foreign policy graduates. Being older and having a wealth of experience not possessed by the young secondary school graduates, they tended to dominate the student bodies of institutes such as MGIMO in the early years and to have the pick of the assignments.

After graduation, the students of the foreign relations institutes were recruited by all the agencies that were short of personnel. Many of the MGIMO graduates simply went into the Ministry of Foreign Affairs, and many of the graduates of the Institute of Foreign Trade entered the Ministry of Foreign Trade. A second important source of employment for the postwar international graduates was journalism. The leading foreign affairs journals, the newspapers, and Tass hired voraciously from the first three or four classes of MGIMO graduates,[17] and then launched them on specialized, internationally oriented careers.

15. This man is Oleg K. Ignatev, the *Pravda* observer for Latin America, Asia, and Africa in 1977. He also reports the relatively minor competition for admission (*nebol'shoi konkurs*) in 1946, a point confirmed in interviews with others. *Altaiskaia pravda*, July 30, 1977, p. 4.

16. *Zhurnalist*, November 1970, p. 61, and June 1976, p. 69.

17. See the articles by the foreign editor of *Izvestiia* at the time, Vladimir Kudriavtsev, in *Zhurnalist*, March 1967, pp. 16–17, and December 1974, p. 29. Biographies of Soviet journalists can be found in *Zhurnalist* since 1967 and in *Molodoi kommunist* since 1973. By the summer of 1977, eighty-six biographies of journalist-internationalists had been found in which the college the person attended was specified. Fifty-six percent graduated from MGIMO, 14 percent from one of the Eastern studies institutes, 6 percent from graduate in-

The journalists covering the other Communist countries were primarily drawn from those reporting the domestic Soviet scene, but those stationed in the non-Communist world in the last thirty years have almost never been shifted between international and domestic reporting. This is even reflected in the term that has regularly been applied to them as a matter of course: *zhurnalist-mezhdunarodnik* (journalist-internationalist). Many of these journalists have moved from one geographic area to another, but they almost always have been assigned to countries where they know the language.

The death of Stalin produced an enormous expansion in the third sphere of employment for the young international graduates—that of scholarly research. At the Twentieth Party Congress in 1956, Khrushchev revised a number of Lenin's central tenets about the capitalist system (for example, the inevitability of war among capitalist states), and later at the congress one of his closest associates, Anastas Mikoyan, pointed out one of the necessary corollaries to this new skepticism about long-established dogmas:

The course of history shows that all the most fundamental propositions of Marxism-Leninism find unceasing confirmation during the present stage of the development of imperialism. But this general confirmation is not enough. We are obligated to study concretely when, where, and to what degree this occurs.

We seriously lag in the study of the contemporary stage of capitalism. We are not engaged in a deep study of facts and figures, but often limit ourselves to seizing upon individual facts as signs of a coming crisis and the impoverishment of the toilers for purposes of propaganda. We do not make a comprehensive and deep evaluation of phenomena which occur in the life of foreign countries.[18]

Shortly after the Twentieth Congress, the Varga Institute was reestablished as the Institute of the World Economy and International Relations (IMEMO) under the USSR Academy of Sciences.[19] Varga was seventy-seven at the time, and the directorship of the institute was given to Anushavan A. Arzumanian, a man with extraordinary political connections. He had been one of the organizers of the Armenian Kom-

---

stitutes of foreign relations (the Higher Diplomatic School or the Institute of the World Economy and International Relations of the Academy of Sciences), 3 percent from the Institute of Foreign Languages, 2 percent from the Institute of Foreign Trade, and 19 percent from all other institutions (half of them from Moscow University).

18. *XX s"ezd Kommunisticheskoi partii Sovetskogo Soiuza [14–25 fevralia 1956]*, *Stenograficheskii otchet* (Moscow: Gospolitizdat, 1956), vol. 1, p. 323.

19. William Zimmerman, *Soviet Perspectives on International Relations, 1956–1967* (Princeton University Press, 1969), pp. 37–39.

somol during the civil war and had then spent years in political work in Armenia. He has especially close ties with Mikoyan; the two men had in fact married sisters. During World War II Arzumanian entered political work in the army and, in retrospect, was fortunate to have been assigned to work in the political department of the Eighteenth Army. The head of the political department was Leonid Brezhnev.[20]

Whether because of its political connections or not, IMEMO prospered after 1956. At the end of that year, it had 170 research associates, including 95 doctors and candidates of science. By January 1974 not only had it increased in size to 572 research associates (including 286 doctors and candidates of science), but at least four of its sections had become independent institutes: the Institute of the USA and Canada, the Institute of the International Workers' Movement, the Institute of Africa, and the Institute of Latin America. These institutes, whose leading officals were often former IMEMO senior scholars, had by that time more than 725 research associates, including 375 doctors and candidates of science.[21]

Scholarship on international subjects was expanded in other parts of the Academy of Sciences as well. The Institute of Oriental Studies, which Mikoyan had severely criticized at the Twentieth Party Congress ("If the entire East has awakened during our time, then this institute still dozes until the present day") was substantially expanded, especially its work on contemporary matters. A new Institute of the Far East (which concentrates on China) was established, and in 1961 an Institute of the Economy of the World Socialist System was formed out of a section of the Institute of Economics.

The rapid expansion in the number and size of the foreign policy institutes created a big personnel problem. Even with the return of some of the older scholars who had (in the words of a later obituary) "worked in the coal industry of Vorkuta [a famous camp],"[22] there were simply not enough scholars to fill the newly created slots. Until the number of degree programs was greatly increased, people were recruited from any likely source. In particular, many journalist-internationalists were drawn into the institutes.

20. *Mirovaia ekonomika i mezhdunarodnye otnosheniia*, May 1974, pp. 117 and 118, contains a description of Arzumanian's career; the information on his wartime experiences is on p. 118.
21. The statistics of this paragraph come from ibid., p. 120.
22. Ibid., April 1977, p. 156.

These men, it should be emphasized, were not simply engaging in academic research. The Ministry of Foreign Affairs has had little research staff, and this apparently is also true of the KGB. The scholarly community working on contemporary problems—and there are some 2,000 to 3,000 of them in Moscow—are supposed to fill the gap. Like scholars everywhere, they are expected to publish books and articles, but those doing policy-relevant work—and there is great pressure to do so—can spend 25 percent of their time or more on classified work usually called "the director's assignments." (The director in question is the director of the institute.) These assignments, which themselves reflect demands or requests from higher authorities, can range from the preparation of a short informational memorandum to a prediction of future developments in the area of their specialization or even to participation in a group working out different policy options for consideration by the Politburo.

The expansion of a scholarly community strongly oriented toward policy questions created another pool of cadres who could be used for other purposes. There was indeed a movement of scholars—though not a large one—into the posts directly involved in policymaking. Economists in particular were sometimes drawn into the Ministry of Foreign Affairs; politically oriented scholars were more often recruited for work in the Central Committee apparatus, especially in the groups of consultants of the Central Committee who work full-time on long-range questions.

Generational Change

In areas like journalism and scholarship, the mass influx of new personnel had an impact upon these institutions almost immediately. Because of the "vacuum" between them and the older specialists, the new recruits moved into middle-level posts earlier than would otherwise have been the case.

The first breakthrough of the younger generation into important leadership posts occurred in the Central Committee apparatus. The secretary heading the international department, Boris Ponomarev (born 1905), retained a number of subordinates who were roughly of his generation. For example, as late as 1979, the deputy head of the international department for Africa was Rostislav Ul'ianovsky, who was born in 1903, and the head of the sector for North America was Nikolai Mostovets, who was born in 1912. But in the Khrushchev period a brain trust (the group of consultants) was created and attached both to the international department and the department for relations with socialist countries and then to the latter alone. The group reported first to the Central Committee secretary, Otto V. Kuusinen, and then in 1964 to his successor, Iurii Andropov. Its first head was Fedor Burlatsky (born 1927), its second, in 1964, Georgii Arbatov (born 1923), and its third, in 1967, Alexander Bovin (born 1930). The international department began to receive younger officials. In particular, Vadim Zagladin (born 1927) became deputy head of the department for Europe in 1967 and then in 1974 the first deputy head of the department, and Karen Brutents, who was born in 1924, became the deputy head for most of the third world.

The second locus of generational change in the foreign policy establishment was the scholarly community. Obviously the great influx of young scholars into the newly created institutes had an impact on them almost immediately, especially because of the near-absence of a middle generation. Already in the early 1960s the young scholars were beginning to become section heads in the institutes, and early in the Brezhnev era they began moving into the directorships. In January 1964 the directors of the institutes of the Academy of Sciences studying the outside world were born in 1907 on the average. By 1969 five of the eight institutes were directed by men born between 1921 and 1928, and a sixth director was born in 1918. The deputy directors of the institutes were almost all born in the 1920s.

The principal figure among the international specialists in the scholarly community was Nikolai Inozemtsev, the director of IMEMO after Arzumanian's death in 1966. When the Institute of the USA and Canada and the Institute of the International Workers' Movement were created out of IMEMO sections, former scholars from IMEMO headed them. Inozemtsev became a candidate member of the Central Committee as early as 1971 and was also named a member of the Presidium of the Academy of Sciences. He was in a key position to influence personnel decisions. In 1978, when the director of the Institute of Oriental Studies died, Inozemtsev was able to have a deputy director of IMEMO appointed as his replacement.[23]

23. E.M. Primakov. His biography is found in *Bol'shaia sovetskaia entsiklopediia* (Moscow: Izdatel'stvo "Sovetskaia entsiklopediia," 1975), vol. 20, p. 582.

Table 6-3. *Average Year of Birth of Officials of the Ministry of Foreign Affairs, 1941–80*

Year	Deputy ministers	Heads of departments	Ambassadors to large countries[a]
January 1941	1884	1905	1906
January 1946	1880	1907	1902
January 1952	1906	1907	1903
January 1957	1908	1909	1907
January 1964	1907	1912	1911
January 1971	1908	1917	1914
January 1977	1912	1919	1918
January 1980	1914	1922	1921

Sources: Individual biographies, most of them drawn from the three editions of *Diplomaticheskii slovar'* (Moscow: Izdatel'stvo politicheskoi, literatury, 1948–50, 1960–64, and 1971–73). For 1980 data, see National Foreign Assessment Center, *Directory of Soviet Officials*, vol. 2: *National Organizations* (Washington, D.C.: Central Intelligence Agency, 1979).
a. Only non-Communist countries with over 15 million population in 1978—a total of thirty-one, although the Soviet Union at no one time had ambassadors in all of them.

A similar generational change occurred among the journalist-internationalists. Good biographical data on the journalists are not available prior to 1967, but since then the data are almost complete.[24] Throughout the 1970s nearly all the important figures covering the international scene—the leading correspondents as well as the foreign editors of the newspapers, Tass, and radio-television—were almost all born later than 1923, and a growing number of the correspondents stationed abroad were born in the 1930s and even in the 1940s. Only among the commentators can members of earlier generations still be found.

Of all the subgroups within the foreign policy establishment, the Ministry of Foreign Affairs was the slowest to undergo generational change. In 1952 the average age of the deputy ministers was forty-five, in 1964 it was fifty-six, and by 1980 it had risen to sixty-five. The heads of the departments of the ministry and the ambassadors to the large non-Communist countries were somewhat younger, but, as table 6-3 indicates, became increasingly older between 1941 and 1980: they averaged thirty-five and thirty-four respectively in 1941 and fifty-seven and fifty-eight in 1980. These middle-level officials tended to be older than their counterparts among international scholars and journalists.

By the late 1970s men born in the middle and late 1920s were begin-

24. See note 17.

ning to rise toward the top and to be interspersed among men of Gromyko's (and Brezhnev's) generation. For example, at present the three deputy ministers of foreign affairs overseeing relations with Africa, the Afghanistan-Iranian area of the Middle East, and Latin America (L.F. Il'ichev, S.P. Kozyrev, and N.S. Ryzhov) average seventy-three years of age, whereas the deputy ministers for the United States and for foreign policy planning (G.M. Kornienko, A.G. Kovalev) are fifty-four and fifty-six respectively.

Because of the pattern of training in the late 1930s and the 1940s, many of the men of the wartime and postwar generations who began to assume important positions came from three or four graduating classes of only a few Moscow institutes. Indeed, a considerable number graduated from a single class, the class of 1949 of the Moscow Institute of International Relations: Vadim Zagladin, the first deputy head of the international department of the Central Committee; Nikolai Inozemtsev, the director of IMEMO; Georgii Arbatov, the director of the Institute of the USA and Canada; the two foreign policy editors of *Pravda* during the Brezhnev period; and a series of middle-level officials.

It is impossible to specify which men will replace the current group of septuagenarians who dominate Soviet foreign policy, but unless very improbable choices are made, the successors will almost surely be ten to fifteen years younger. The minister of foreign affairs was born in 1909, his first deputy ministers in 1917 and 1925 (and the latter is the man in charge of relations with the West and the Middle East); the head of the international department of the Central Committee was born in 1905 and his first deputy in 1928; the minister of foreign trade was born in 1908 and his new first deputy in 1933; the deputy chairman of the Council of Ministers in charge of foreign economic policy was born in 1907 and the deputy chairman representing the Soviet Union in the Council of Economic Mutual-Assistance (the agency coordinating economic plans with East Europe) was born in 1928; the minister of defense was born in 1908 and his first deputy ministers in 1914, 1918, and 1921 (and the younger two are more important than the older one). If the leadership wants important new officials with foreign policy experience who come from the 1910–18 generation, it can find a few (for example, Mikhail Zimianin, the Central Committee secretary in charge of ideological questions), but probably by the early 1980s the top Soviet foreign policy elite will have undergone a near-complete transformation. A strong majority of the new elite will have been selected from members of the wartime and postwar generations—men whose work experience will have taken place largely in the post-Stalin period.

Generational Differences in Attitude

In analyzing the attitudes of most of the Soviet specialized elites, one is often driven to speculate on relatively weak data. For the foreign policy specialists, however, much better evidence exists. The scholars and quite a few Central Committee officials write articles that often express differences of opinion or imply different assumptions about the outside world. Because this is also an elite with whom Westerners have a good deal of personal contact, it is possible to gain some feeling about differences within the group.

If one carefully analyzed the foreign policy debates over a long period, one obviously would not find total uniformity of views among those of any age. There are nonconventional thinkers among members of the Brezhnev generation and very traditional analysts among the postwar generation. Nevertheless, the generational difference in attitudes is striking, and relatively young Soviet scholars acknowledge and discuss it freely.

Basically, for all their growth in sophistication, the older specialists on the outside world have found it very difficult to free themselves from the set of ideas they developed when young. Those who had worked with Varga before the closing of his institute in 1949 and had shared his views had, of course, no difficulty in breaking away from the most primitive dogmas of the late-Stalin period. Indeed, they delighted in obtaining revenge in the late 1950s and early 1960s. Yet it is striking how many of the leading innovators of the 1950s and early 1960s became relatively conservative figures in the 1970s. They had not changed their earlier views, whereas younger scholars began moving beyond them and conceptualizing the outside world in different terms.

The differences between the generations are difficult to explain succinctly to an audience that is unfamiliar with the Soviet terms of debate. In general, the traditional Leninist view had treated "capitalism" or "imperialism" (an exact synonym for advanced capitalism) almost as a living thing—as a monster reaching its tentacles into the colonial world. (The parallels with the American image of "totalitarianism" are striking.)

Specialists of the postwar generation, on the other hand, are unlikely to even use the word *imperialism* as the subject of a sentence, especially if they are specialists on the United States or Western Europe. The younger scholars see the world in more differentiated terms and are likely to find local explanations for an event rather than blame it on the machinations of the imperialists. Specialists on Latin America, for example, study not only American policy toward Latin America, but also relations between Brazil and Argentina, and so forth. They do not simply explain the overthrow of Allende by the American intervention, but rather emphasize Chilean internal factors. In the process, political explanations for events tend to be much more prominent in analyses made by the postwar generation, especially those under forty-five.[25]

In fact, the attitude of the postwar generation toward the outside world tends to be different from that of its predecessors. The older generation often came to international studies through an interest in and dedication to the international Communist movement. Emotional commitment was as important as curiosity in guiding their work, and many worked in the Comintern or its institutes. Members of the younger generation, by contrast, often chose their careers because of their fascination with the West and their desire to travel abroad. The scholars among them who arose within the system of the Academy of Sciences are driven more by simple intellectual curiosity. Instead of being absorbed in thoughts about how to promote change in the West, they are more likely to wonder which aspects of Western development have or ought to have relevance for the Soviet future.

To the extent that the middle-aged and younger members of the foreign policy establishment tend to be modernizers—and even Westernizers—in Soviet politics, they tend to be strong supporters of détente. They have a sense that xenophobia and cold war relations with the West are associated with reaction at home—with a fundamentalist, ultranationalist mentality that bodes no good for them personally or for the values to which they adhere.

25. See Jerry F. Hough, "The Evolution in the Soviet World View," *World Politics*, vol. 32 (July 1980), and Jerry F. Hough, "The Evolving Soviet Debates on Latin America," *Latin American Research Review*, forthcoming.

The attitudes of diplomats, KGB agents, and journalists are harder to document, for the first two groups do not publish and the third serves propagandistic purposes. But no one who has met the younger men working in these occupations in the West has failed to be impressed by the degree of their fascination with Western culture and fashion, by their attraction to inside-dopester political explanations for events.

The postwar generation of foreign policy specialists is not, of course, composed largely of passivists or of people who believe that the Soviet Union should function as a small, uninvolved power. Those who are inclined to think that way are as unlikely to be chosen for top positions as their counterparts in the United States. The basic viewpoint of these specialists remains Marxist, and when the outside world seems threatening, they often appear to fall back on more traditional images. At these times they see policy determined by the "ruling circles" in the United States, and in a paranoid way they sometimes seem to betray an anxiety that "ruling circles" and "forces hostile to the Soviet Union" are synonymous. Even an extremely sophisticated scholar may state with pride that he has come to understand that power is not concentrated in many of the places that were emphasized by Marxists in the past, but then he may admit that he still does not know precisely where it is located—and do so in a manner that suggests he believes there is such a place.

Yet it is a Marxism that fully accepts Varga's judgments about the ability of capitalism to survive for a long time. (As Inozemtsev, the director of IMEMO, said in 1970, life "again and again" shows that Varga was correct.)[26] It is a Marxism that is trying to come to grips with the fact that big businessmen seem more favorable to détente than many other groups in the United States and that these businessmen lose on such issues as the Jackson-Vanik Amendment to the Trade Act of 1974, with the fact that statistical studies seem to show that high military expenditures are associated with higher unemployment than lower, and so forth.

No Soviet leadership—in fact, no leadership in Russia, regardless of the nature of the political system in that country—is going to usher in a period of bliss in Russian-American relations, for the world remains sufficiently bipolar to produce strains and suspicions, whoever the leaders are on each side. The next Soviet leader will almost surely

26. *Mirovaia ekonomika i mezhdunarodnye otnosheniia*, January 1970, p. 124.

not be drawn from the foreign policy specialists, and his basic values will be determined by forces within the party leadership and within society as a whole rather than by those within the foreign policy establishment. Nevertheless, his chief advisers and policymaking lieutenants in the foreign policy realm will almost surely be men who are considerably younger than their predecessors. Instead of having had little exposure to the West in their twenties and thirties (or even later) and of having worked for decades in the stultifying atmosphere of the rigid Stalin ideology, they will be men who have studied the West for decades, who have traveled extensively, and who seem more interested in the benefits of cooperation than in scoring points in a competition with the United States. It is difficult to believe that this will not create the possibility for some change in Soviet behavior, at least if the external environment permits it.

7

Economic Reform

FOR OVER sixty years Westerners have been talking about the difficulties in the Soviet economy, about the mistakes inherent in socialist planning, and, indeed, in the case of some analysts, about its imminent stagnation or even collapse. Yet in the broad historical perspective the Soviet economy has performed rather well, especially given its relative lack of foreign investment and the large proportion of its resources devoted to military purposes. The Soviet Union has moved from being a quite underdeveloped country to one capable of outstanding accomplishments in space. Its rate of economic growth, even in the "slowdown" of the 1970s, has been substantial, well above that of the United States. In the thirty-five years since the end of World War II, the consumer has enjoyed a steadily rising standard of living.

Even some of the defects in the Soviet economy most noted in the West take on a somewhat different meaning when one remembers that the Soviet Union has been a developing country. Such countries are seldom strong in technological innovation, but instead rationally copy or import the technology developed in more advanced countries. (Twenty-five years ago Japan was renowned for the low-quality, imitative consumer goods it exported.) Developing countries normally have very high unemployment rates in the city; therefore, the employment of excess labor by the industrial enterprises in the Soviet Union helps to solve a large social problem. Such countries often have extremes in social wealth, with a drain of capital to Swiss banks and of young brains to the West. Nonconvertibility of currency and tight restrictions on emigration from the Soviet Union force the well-to-do and the upper-middle class to direct their energies into improving the local economy. The underdeveloped consumer sector and the pricing of many basic items below cost in the Soviet Union lead to shortages and lines that necessarily create pressure for equality not found in a country like, for example, Brazil.

The main economic problem in the Soviet Union is that it is no long-

Table 7-1. *Estimated Number of Eighteen-Year-Old Males Available for the Economy and the Military, 1975–90*
Millions

Year	Men reaching age eighteen[a]	Men available for the draft[b]
1975	2.493	1.948
1976	2.558	2.008
1977	2.605	2.051
1978	2.646	2.086
1979	2.637	2.080
1980	2.542	1.993
1981	2.432	1.896
1982	2.308	1.785
1983	2.173	1.658
1984	2.106	1.592
1985	2.062	1.545
1986	2.020	1.495
1987	2.012	1.489
1988	2.034	1.507
1989	2.097	1.560
1990	2.142	1.600

Source: Murray Feshbach and Stephen Rapawy, "Soviet Population and Manpower Trends and Policies," in *Soviet Economy in a New Perspective: A Compendium of Papers Submitted to the Joint Economic Committee*, 94 Cong., 2 sess. (GPO, 1976), p. 150.
a. The number of eighteen-year-old women is virtually identical.
b. This calculation takes into account the effect of deferments and exemptions. The annual number of conscriptees at the present time is estimated at 1,688,000.

er underdeveloped. The economy has become much larger and more complex, and the amount of work involved in specifying suppliers, prices, the assortment of goods produced, their recipients, wages, and so forth has grown geometrically as the number of plants, items manufactured, and labor specialties have increased. Moreover, as Japanese experience (and also American experience at the turn of the century) suggests, there comes a point when a well-functioning economy should become less imitative and more innovative. There comes a point when the most serious labor problem is not the utilization of an excessive number of new arrivals from the countryside, but the efficient employment of a trained urban labor force.

In general terms, the Soviet economy has reached these points. The issue has been brought sharply to the fore by a major demographic change that will occur in the early 1980s. The birthrate in the Soviet Union during World War II was very low, and when these war babies grew up, they inevitably produced an abnormally small number of children. In the 1980s these children of the World War II babies will become adults, and as a result, the labor force will receive a very small "entering class." The number of eighteen-year-olds in the mid-1980s will be from 20 to 25 percent smaller than it was in the late 1970s (see table 7-1).

This development will occur at a time when the flow of people from the countryside into the city is beginning to dry up and the percentage of women working in the labor force is near its peak. (Virtually all able-bodied women are employed or in school, and as the country becomes more prosperous many can afford to become housewives or part-time employees, especially when they have small children—and many want to do so.) Soviet specialists have calculated that the urban labor force will experience only a small increase in the 1980s and that nearly all the economic growth will have to come from increases in labor productivity. In addition, of course, the energy crisis—and the coming topping-out of Soviet petroleum production—creates great pressure for an increase in efficiency.

The fact that an economic problem exists is widely recognized in the Soviet Union. In interviews, officials of the State Committee on Labor and Social Problems, the Central Trade Union Council, the Young Communist League, and two important economic institutes all brought up the question of the labor shortage on their own.[1] Liberal economists have insisted for years that the problems of detailed central planning would grow progressively worse as the economy became more complex and the number of transactions to be planned increased. In November 1978 Brezhnev himself—in the most outspoken speech on the economy he is ever known to have given—discussed almost all these criticisms:

From the beginning of the 80s, we will have to put even greater reliance on intensive factors of economic growth, for other factors will be sharply restricted. . . .

[There are] shortages of metal and fuel . . . a certain lag of machinery from the needs of the economy . . . the failure of the construction plan to be completed [and] intolerable losses of grain, fruit, and vegetables. . . . A complex situation has developed in transportation, especially in the railroads [which] all of you, I suppose, feel directly. . . .

1. Jerry F. Hough, "Policy Making and the Worker," in Arcadius Kahan and Blair A. Ruble, eds., *Industrial Labor in the U.S.S.R.* (Elmsford, N.Y.: Pergamon Press, 1979), pp. 367–96.

Some officials of the planning and economic organs continue to look at the consumers' industries as some kind of balancer. By cutting investment in them, they try to overcome any imbalances that appear in the plan. . . .

What explains the fact that . . . we cannot avoid those bottlenecks which do not permit us to go forward more quickly and dynamically. . . . The chief reason is that the central economic organs, the ministries, and the departments have been slow in achieving a transition to intensive development. They have not been able to achieve the necessary improvement of qualitative indicators or the speeding-up of scientific-technical progress.[2]

There is also widespread agreement in the Soviet Union that there should be "an improvement in the plans, accompanied by measures for perfecting the whole economic mechanism."[3] But how should this be done? When petroleum becomes scarcer, the natural tendency is to issue central directives ordering greater conservation; when a labor shortage is impending, the natural response is to create yet another plan indicator limiting the number of workers that a plant manager can hire. A number of economists, however, insist that the answer is not more centralized control but less. They suggest that managers should be given more independence and that such economic indicators as profit be used more extensively to control their behavior.

The issue of economic reform is in many ways the central one in the Soviet political system at the present time. It is complex in its own right, for neither the optimal extent to which market mechanisms should be used nor the proper indicators to use are at all self-evident. Moreover, the issue touches on the power of nearly all the important institutions in Soviet society and has implications for nearly all the other sensitive questions in Soviet politics.

Philosophical and Social Issues

When Americans talk about the obstacles to economic reform in the Soviet Union, they often refer to "ideology." Presumably it is thought that the Marxist-Leninist abhorrence of capitalism makes an economic reform utilizing market mechanisms unthinkable. In some cases this

2. *Pravda*, November 28, 1978, pp. 1–2. A number of Brezhnev's speeches were not published at the time, but lengthy excerpts from most of them were later reprinted in volumes presenting his views on selected topics. None of these speeches published later had the tone of his 1978 speech.

3. Ibid., p. 2.

may be true. For example, Khrushchev stated in his memoirs that in 1955 Mikhail Suslov even opposed reconciliation with Yugoslavia because it was not really socialist.[4] And conceivably, many people still have a rigid sense of what is and is not real socialism.

Nevertheless, a generalized ideological impact on economic reform should not be exaggerated, for Marxism-Leninism has proved to be relatively flexible. The private plot, and the free peasant market that goes with it, has existed for a long time, and the Brezhnev regime has moved to give it added legitimacy. Even dacha owners are now being pressured to have their fruit and vegetable gardens. The desirability of incentive systems has been loudly proclaimed since the 1930s, and no one suggests—in print at least—that Yugoslavia, let alone Poland and Hungary, is not socialist.

Although the various arguments against major economic reform—and the degree of support for them—are often influenced by the Marxist-Leninist ideology, they are very practical.

The first question about economic reform, of course, is whether it will work. Sometimes even Americans who are highly critical of Milton Friedman's prescriptions for U.S. economic policy take it for granted that the introduction of market mechanisms would automatically solve all problems in the Soviet Union. Clearly they would not. Corporations in the United States do not give their plant managers much freedom in setting prices, in designing the product, in deciding how much to produce, and in making important investment decisions. The great strength of capitalism has been that people with ideas have had the freedom to develop new products and establish new firms if they can find financing. It will not be easy to introduce that advantage into a system in which all the major factories are nationalized.

The second question raised about economic reform concerns its social consequences. Even in a country like the United States where market mechanisms are constantly praised, recent public opinion polls show majority support for wage and price controls and widespread skepticism about the ability of the "invisible hand" to control managerial decisions about prices. It is scarcely surprising that Russians, who have not heard the market commended, are inclined to fear that a loos-

4. Nikita S. Khrushchev, *Khrushchev Remembers*, trans. and ed. Strobe Talbott (Little, Brown, 1970), p. 377.

ening of controls on managers will result in prices going up. Certainly nothing in the Yugoslavian experience with inflation discourages such a view.

There is also a fear that meaningful economic reform will cause unemployment. Developing countries are often characterized by high rates of urban unemployment—as, indeed, was the Soviet Union during the period of the New Economic Policy in the 1920s. Since 1930, however, the policy of rapid industrialization, coupled with incentives for managers to hire as much labor as possible, has created not only full employment but a persistent labor shortage. This feature of Soviet society has been much emphasized in internal propaganda. In recent years, when Soviet newspapers have replied to the Carter administration's human rights campaign, the most frequent reference was to the right to work (really the guarantee of a job) in the Soviet Union as opposed to the insecurity produced by unemployment in the West. Managerial freedom and incentive to economize on labor means that people are discharged, and this gives rise to concern.

Finally, concern is expressed about the impact of economic reform upon equality in income and services. Americans seem enthralled with the existence of privilege in the Soviet Union, and every new correspondent in Moscow rediscovers it to the delight of his or her readers. In comparative perspective, however, the level of privileges of the top Soviet 10,000—which is essentially the group on which Hedrick Smith focuses in *The Russians*—is not remotely in the same league as that of the top 10,000 in America. Over a twenty-five-year period, there has been a strong trend in the Soviet Union toward equalizing income distribution and toward lessening the gap between city and country life.[5]

But everything has its costs. Leading Soviet economists are now proclaiming—both privately and in print—that income distribution in the Soviet Union is more egalitarian than in most Eastern European countries and that, as a result, the monetary incentives for the productive and the innovative have become too small to serve as effective stimuli. These economists are calling for an increase in incentive differentials—sometimes a sharp increase.

A number of objections have been raised to these arguments. What-

5. See the superb study by Alastair McAuley, *Economic Welfare in the Soviet Union* (University of Wisconsin Press, 1979).

ever the degree of equality in income distribution today in comparison with that in the past—or with that in the West—many social problems still exist, each having its advocates for specific policy actions. An improvement of conditions in the countryside, more subsidized day-care centers, reduced work hours for women, more money for the poor—all these proposals are expensive, and all compete with proposals to increase the money going into economic incentives.

Other objections are political. Not far beneath the surface, of course, is always the fear that decentralization of authority will somehow lead to a fatal loss of political control in the non-Russian republics. A more immediate problem stems from the fact that the decentralization of authority will be counterproductive unless price relationships push managers to decisions that are optimal from the national point of view. In practice, many prices are not economically rational and therefore give a freer manager the incentive to take actions that are irrational from the standpoint of the economy. Some basic consumer items (for example, meat) are sold below cost. If the prices of some politically sensitive goods were to be increased at a time when the lower-income groups were receiving little in the way of wage increases, the political dangers are clear, even to someone who does not remember the meat riots in Poland that brought down Wladyslaw Gomulka.

The obvious solution to the problem of increasing the relative share of the rewards given to the most productive while still permitting an absolute increase in the share going to the poor would be to reduce military expenditures. This solution would be all the more attractive because of the impending labor shortage in the 1980s among those of draft age. However, if the military perceives economic reform to be contrary to its basic interests, it can certainly be expected to oppose reform.

Naturally, not all the arguments about economic reform are on one side of the debate. The military, for example, is aware that military power at present depends upon economic growth and the ability of the economy to innovate. A reduction in the size of the army might not seem so intolerable if it promised a better-functioning economy (and especially if it were accompanied by a lessening threat from China). Similarly, the ideological distaste for market mechanisms may be reduced by an even greater distaste for the illegal and semilegal markets—the "second economy"—that must generate concern about their impact on the moral fiber of society. The political danger of economic reform may be considered less threatening than the danger of no reform. Brezhnev himself raised this point in talking about the "intolerable losses" of fruits and vegetables in the trade system. "Today with full justification we say that this question . . . is not simply an economic one. It is also a major political question, for it directly influences the mood and labor activity of the Soviet people."[6]

The fundamental political strength of economic reform is that it would tend to benefit the most skilled and the best educated. Not only would they receive more income, but because they can afford to buy sophisticated consumer goods and to go to restaurants, they would gain most from an improved consumer and service sector. Such people would have little fear of unemployment, and their fears about inflation could be alleviated by a policy of indexing pensions. Since they have every incentive to think of reasons why reform would serve the interests of others and of the economy as a whole, it is difficult to believe that they will not do so. The combination of a demographic problem and an energy crisis will provide them with a golden opportunity to make the case for greater efficiency.

Institutional Conflicts

In no country is politics simply a conflict between abstract philosophical principles or social policies. Instead these principles and policies become associated with institutional interests and social forces; the victory or defeat of the principles depends in large part on the strength of the forces behind them.

In analyzing the politics of economic reform, Westerners have often described the party apparatus and the governmental administration as the two great institutional protagonists. As Leonard Schapiro wrote, "By and large, the views that favor discipline, centralized controls, and absolute priority for heavy industry can be regarded as those of the party apparatus, while the views that look toward greater reliance on material incentives, increased application of market principles, decentralization of industrial controls, and higher priority for consumer goods can be identified with the government apparatus, including the

6. *Pravda*, November 28, 1978, p. 2.

planners and managers."[7] A Soviet refugee, Alexander Yanow, presents a similar view in a recent monograph in which he contrasts the progressive managers with the conservative local party officials.[8]

Despite the popularity of this view, it is open to serious questions. In the first place, of course, neither the officials of the state bureaucracy nor those in the party apparatus can all have identical views. Both include officials between the ages of thirty and seventy who have a variety of occupations and responsibilities. In the state apparatus, for example, Schapiro's "planners and managers" include top officials of the State Planning Committee (Gosplan) and factory managers, and all the evidence suggests that they have divergent opinions about the proper role and power of Gosplan.

In general, the central governmental administration is not the chief proponent of market principles and decentralization of industrial controls, but their chief opponent. Gosplan, which has the right to confirm (or reject) a remarkable number of decisions made by other institutions, is not volunteering to surrender these rights. On the contrary, when the Gosplan deputy chairman for labor and wages gave his solution to the impending labor shortage, it was to give Gosplan greater control over the number of workers permitted in each plant.[9] Similarly, the Ministry of Finances, which is responsible for establishing the size of administrative and professional staffs of agencies and enterprises and of enforcing these regulations, does not favor abrogating these controls. The State Committee for Labor and Social Problems tends to favor the principle of nationwide uniformity of wages for work of similar nature in similar climatic conditions, perhaps because the uniform wage scales are worked on in the state committee. The ministries, of course, believe that the economic system would function more efficiently if the limitations on their freedom by Gosplan, the State Committee on Labor and Social Problems, and others were reduced, but strangely they do not seem sympathetic about complaints by plant managers that ministerial limitations on *their* freedom are counterproductive.

7. Leonard Schapiro, "Keynote—Compromise," *Problems of Communism*, vol. 20 (July–August 1971), p. 2.

8. Alexander Yanov, *Détente after Brezhnev: The Domestic Roots of Soviet Foreign Policy*, trans. Robert Kessler, Policy Papers in International Affairs: No. 1 (University of California Institute of International Studies, 1977), pp. 28–30, 38–39.

9. A. Bachurin, "Zadachi uskoreniia rosta proizvoditel'nosti truda," *Voprosy ekonomiki*, August 1978, pp. 3–14.

The position of the local managers—that is, the industrial plant managers—appears somewhat schizophrenic. On the one hand, for years their articles have appealed for greater freedom for themselves in many areas. On the other hand, they continually complain that firm annual plans are not established a year in advance and that the supply system is not sufficiently predictable and reliable in its operation. That greater managerial freedom might lead to greater unpredictability for other managers is a question they never seriously discuss.

It is unclear how important the views of the plant managers are in the politics of economic reform. The manager of a major plant can be a powerful force in local politics, for his plant's performance is crucial in the central evaluation of local party officials and the plant is an important factor in housing and municipal construction. If the city centers largely on one plant, it can conceivably function as a company town.[10] But the importance of plant managers in national politics is more problematical. If on the basis of their specialized knowledge they can persuade the leadership of the desirability of some reform, they may have a great impact. However, in assessing their independent power and authority, one should not forget that the director of a Soviet automobile plant is comparable to the director of a General Motors assembly plant, not to the president of General Motors.

The provincial party secretaries, however, are much more substantial figures in national politics, and their opinions on economic reform are of prime importance. They are drawn from a variety of professions and work in urban and rural areas in Russian and non-Russian territories. Their views, no doubt, reflect this diversity. Nevertheless, it is difficult to believe that, even on the average, there is a sharp dichotomy between the urban party officials and the plant managers on the issue of economic reform.

Those who have examined Soviet biographical data closely have concluded that Soviet officials on the rise often move back and forth between posts in the party and state apparatuses, but that they seldom—at least in the postwar period—move across functional lines. A factory manager may become (with an intervening party post) the Central Committee secretary for heavy industry, and a second secretary of the Kazakhstan Central Committee may become the USSR Minister of

10. William Taubman, *Governing Soviet Cities: Bureaucratic Politics and Urban Development in the USSR* (Praeger, 1973), esp. pp. 54–72.

Agriculture. In fact, in mid-1980 the two national officials in question have precisely this background. However, an official handling agriculture in either the party or state hierarchy would almost never be switched to industrial responsibilities, except in rare cases in the food industry. As John Armstrong wrote, "It is clear that career divisions within both the state bureaucracy and the party bureaucracy are much more significant than the division between these bureaucracies. In fact, there is such a high degree of interchange between the middle levels of the state and party bureaucracies that it is impossible to look upon these organizations as separate elite segments."[11]

In short, instead of separate party and state hierarchies being the main political actors, the Soviet political system really features numerous complexes and subcomplexes that cut across the formal institutions. (The word *complex* is being used as it is in the phrase "military-industrial complex," to denote officials in different institutions who have similar enough interests to form an important political group.) The complexes include not only the party and governmental officials with similar backgrounds and functional responsibilities, but the specialized officials of Gosplan, the trade unions, the Young Communist League, and so on.

For purposes of this analysis, the important thing to understand is that the top secretaries of the party committees of large cities and the managers of heavy industry plants tend to be part of the same complex, especially in the Russian and the Ukraine republics. The first secretaries of the city party committees in these republics have habitually been engineers with some industrial experience, but the first secretaries newly elected in the 1970s had even more industrial experience than their predecessors. In the other republics, where city first secretaries had often been men with teaching and Young Communist League experience (experience no doubt thought useful in training officials to deal with sensitive nationality questions), the pattern of appointments has become increasingly like that in the RSFSR and the Ukraine (see table 7-2). As the major regions (equivalent to American states) have become more industrialized, their first secretaries too have been increasingly recruited from the ranks of those with engi-

11. John A. Armstrong, *The Soviet Bureaucratic Elite: A Case Study of the Ukrainian Apparatus* (Praeger, 1959), p. 144. See also Grey Hodnett, *Leadership in the Soviet National Republics* (Oakville, Ontario: Mosaic Press, 1978), pp. 35–36.

Table 7-2. *Characteristics of City Party First Secretaries in Cities with over 100,000 Population*
Percent

| | Year in which first selected | | |
Characteristic	1957–64	1965–70	1971–80
Russian Republic[a]			
Engineering education	81	76	86
At least five years work in industry[b]	67	73	84
At least ten years work in industry[b]	36	38	64
Other republics[c]			
Engineering education	38	50	60
At least five years work in industry[b]	23	30	50
At least ten years work in industry[b]	23	20	30

Sources: Individual biographies from various Soviet sources.
a. Excludes the autonomous republics in the RSFSR, because of lack of sufficient numbers. The meager evidence suggests that the pattern in the autonomous republics may be more like that in the other union republics. The figures are based on fifty-eight secretaries in 1957–64, twenty-nine secretaries in 1965–70, and thirty-six secretaries in 1971–80.
b. Includes construction, transportation, and geology.
c. Excludes the Ukraine, because of lack of sufficient numbers. The meager evidence suggests that the pattern in the Ukraine may be more like that in the RSFSR. The figures are based on thirteen secretaries in 1957–64, twenty secretaries in 1965–70, and ten secretaries in 1971–80.

Table 7-3. *Characteristics of Regional Party First Secretaries in the Thirty-three Most Populous Regions, 1950–80[a]*
Percent

Characteristic	1950	1960	1966	1980
Engineering education	38	44	55	61
At least five years work in industry[b]	14	32	42	57
At least ten years work in industry[b]	0	23	33	29
Previously first secretary of a city party committee[c]	28	42	45	63

Sources: Individual biographies from various Soviet sources.
a. Regions with over 2 million people in 1978.
b. Includes construction and transportation.
c. In the second half of the 1940s, the first secretaries of the regional party committees simultaneously held the post of first secretary of the city party committee of the regional capital. In practice, the second secretary of the city committee of the capital served as the party leader on day-to-day questions, and men who held this post are counted as first secretary during those years.

neering degrees and experience both in industrial management and urban party work (see table 7-3).

Even if the general background and perspective of a former managerial official in a party post is similar to that of managerial personnel still in industry, their specific responsibilities obviously create divergent interests between them on a number of issues. Because the city party officials are responsible for the city as a whole, they frequently must choose between the demands of different institutions and plants in the city or make demands on any one of them. Moreover, effective city planning is complicated by the fact that a large proportion of the funds for housing and municipal construction are funneled into the city through the industrial ministries. Any attempt by the city officials to promote integrated urban development requires pressure on the managers to take into account citywide as well as parochial needs.

On the question of economic reform, however, the interests of the plant managers and the local party secretaries are much closer. Articles by the secretaries are filled with complaints about ministerial and Gosplan investment decisions—especially of the indifference to well-balanced regional development. The secretaries can appeal to the central party organs to try to force a ministry to make a particular decision, but they have no authority over the ministries. By contrast, they do have the power to compel a local administrator, including a plant manager, to take actions that are within his legal authority. As a result, the greater the independence of the plant manager from ministerial control, the greater the potential influence of local party officials on his decisions. The more investment decisions made by officials at a local level, the greater the ability of the local party officials to shape them in a way that takes regional needs into account.

Furthermore, the logic of the command economy has driven local party officials into detailed and onerous work in the area of supplies procurement. In his memoirs Brezhnev reported a case in which he, as first secretary of an important region, had appealed in 1947 or 1948 to the number-two man in the political system, Andrei Zhdanov, for help in obtaining light bulbs.[12] Although the role of the local party organs in this type of supplies procurement and institutional mediation is functional for the economy as it is now organized, men who are mayors of cities and governors of states like to see their role in grander terms. They would much prefer to spend their time organizing and implementing large development plans. The regional first secretaries, almost all of whom are members of the Central Committee, would like to spend more time functioning as national politicians.

12. L. I. Brezhnev, "Vozrozhdenie," *Novyi mir*, no. 5 (May 1978), p. 15.

Generational Change and Economic Reform

To a great extent the politics of economic reform tends to have an institutional rather than a generational character. The fact that major institutions would have their power affected in important ways obviously influences the opinions and political activity of their top officials. Younger officials of Gosplan are, on the whole, unlikely to favor a reduction in Gosplan's power, whereas older plant managers are likely to favor an increase in their own independence. Ministerial officials are inclined to think that good results can be obtained by administrative decrees (and often only by this means), whereas economists are apt to think that economic levers are more effective. Of course, if the economists work in a Gosplan institute, they would be better advised not to appeal too vigorously in print for a reduction in Gosplan's role.

Nevertheless, the generational factor is still important in the politics of economic reform. Any conflict between ministers and plant managers, between Gosplan deputy chairmen and local party officials, is predominantly one between men in their sixties or even older and men in their fifties or late forties (see table 7-4). Those pushing economic reform can regard ministerial and Gosplan opposition as that of old and out-of-touch men who are desperately trying to hang on to the only kind of administrative system within which they are able to function. And these advocates can regard economic reform as something that will facilitate the retirement of the Brezhnev and 1910–18 generations and that will open up occupational mobility for themselves.

Besides a generational difference in self-interest among fairly high level officials, there is, on balance, surely a generational difference in values. In the late 1920s and early 1930s Stalin suppressed empirical and quantitative economics as a discipline. Not only did the future administrators fail to receive any significant economic training as part of their engineering and agronomy education, but no young professional economists with a mathematical background—and relatively few political economists—were trained.

In the Khrushchev years the situation changed radically. The leadership denounced the earlier neglect of economics and called for its rapid development. A separate discipline of mathematical economics was established to supplement traditional political economy, and a growing number of research institutes and university departments were created

Table 7-4. *Average Age of Industrial-Construction Ministers and RSFSR Plant Managers, 1950–80*[a]

Year	Industrial-construction ministers	Managers of large plants[b]
January 1950	46	42
	(27)	(56)
January 1957	50	48
	(28)	(72)
January 1966	56	51
	(33)	(86)
January 1980	66	50
	(42)	(77)

Sources: Biographical and age data from the regional press and scattered sources.

a. The figures in parentheses indicate the number of officials included in each group.

b. Large plants include the 170 largest plants as defined in Jerry F. Hough, *The Soviet Prefects* (Harvard University Press, 1969), pp. 335–40, plus newer plants and defense plants that seem to be of comparable size.

to utilize and teach it. Although the mathematical economists have been split among several schools, their views on the whole have been strikingly different from those of the old-time political economists. As Richard Judy stated in 1971 after a comprehensive survey of the positions taken by economists in the economic debates of the 1960s, "the positions of any Soviet economist can be predicted with considerable accuracy if information is available on his age, his organization of primary affiliation, and his degree of mathematical proficiency":

There is a strong correlation between the ages of Soviet economists and their positions on questions of economic policy, theory, and methodology. Three age groups are distinguishable:

1. The pre-revolutionary generation of economists who were born before 1900. They were young adults in 1917 [and] many participated in the remarkably creative developments in economics during the 1920s. . . .

2. The Stalinist generation consists of people who were born in this century before 1917. Most numerous are those born in the decade 1900–1909. These men were under thirty years of age when Stalin's purges of analytical economists began in 1930. Many advanced rapidly to responsible positions in the 1930s. Their formative years were those of the purges and of great emphasis on ideological doctrine.

3. The post-revolutionary generation was born in 1917 or after. These men had only indirect contact with the purges of the 1930s. They grew up in a Stalinist environment but most were under thirty when Stalin died in 1953. They were young enough to adapt rapidly to the changing demands placed before Soviet economists after 1955.[13]

13. Richard W. Judy, "The Economists," in H. Gordon Skilling and Franklyn Griffiths, eds., *Interest Groups in Soviet Politics* (Princeton University Press, 1971), pp. 250, 216.

Since this was written, the only changes have been the passing of the prerevolutionary generation and of course a large increase in the number of economists with the "younger" attitudes and education.

The Khrushchev and Brezhnev regimes also made a great effort to diffuse an economic perspective more widely through the administrative elite. In the Khrushchev era the system of part-time party education, in which virtually all party members are required to enroll, centered on empirical economics rather than the party history and Marxist-Leninist philosophy that were the core of the curriculum in the Stalin years. In the post-Khrushchev period the system of party education itself became more balanced in its coverage, but the party instituted a wide range of short-term, mid-career courses for managers, one of whose purposes was to periodically broaden the economic perspective of managers trained as engineers. Also, the engineering education in the colleges was given a heavier economic component.

Obviously these changes should not be exaggerated. Gertrude Schroeder is right to remind us that all the participants in the published economic debates are "conservatives" in the sense that they seek to have their reforms carried out within a system of state ownership and central planning.[14] Moreover, a number of the mathematical economists retain the faith—or at least the hope—that computers can serve as a substitute for the market in determining rational prices and the decisions based upon them.[15] Similarly, mass programs on economics in the Soviet Union deal with cost-cutting far more than with the propagation of market economics.

Nevertheless, a fundamental change has occurred. Suslov's 1955 opposition to the reconciliation with Yugoslavia on the ground that the Yugoslavian economy simply was not socialistic must have reflected a widespread feeling among members of his generation. But twenty years of propaganda that has treated the use of economic levers in laudatory terms must have eroded this kind of attitude, especially among the young and the middle-aged. Although doubts certainly continue to exist about the effectiveness of this or that concrete economic reform,

14. Gertrude E. Schroeder, "The Soviet Economy on a Treadmill of 'Reforms,' " in *Soviet Economy in a Time of Change*, Joint Economic Committee print, 96 Cong. 1 sess. (Government Printing Office, 1979), vol. 1, p. 339.

15. Aron Katsenelinboigen, *Studies in Soviet Economic Planning* (White Plains, N.Y.: M. E. Sharpe, 1978), pp. 48–74.

the concept of economic reform now conveys the image of modernity rather than of ideological deviation.

Such an attitude is apt to be found not just among the pragmatists of the young and middle-aged generations, but among the ideologues. Those who are seriously interested in Marxism-Leninism tend to be attracted less to its dogmas than to Marx's ideas about alienation and a just society. Such men are apt to be less concerned about the lack of orthodoxy in economic reform than about its impact on egalitarian social policies. Even they, however, are likely to be concerned about the moral consequences of a growing black-and-gray market and to be attracted to the argument that a reform which will undercut this illicit market is important for the health of society.

In other respects, too, age is likely to be correlated with attitudes toward economic reform. Within the military, as has been seen, the older generation of commanders was conditioned to treat manpower as cheap and technology as expensive. The young and middle-aged commanders have been trained to reverse this set of priorities; they are therefore far more likely to be sympathetic to the argument that Soviet military power ultimately rests on the society's ability to produce technological innovation. In a period of fewer eighteen-year-olds, the younger commanders must surely see an industry that is wasteful of labor as a deadly competitor to the military for manpower and must feel favorable to measures that induce plant managers to economize on labor.

Within the educated and skilled population as a whole, the relatively young do not have memories of conditions in the 1910s and 1920s with which to compare present standards of living. Increasingly their bases of comparison come from the post-Stalin period, so that they are less impressed than older people by the degree of change that has occurred in their adult lives. The superelite of Hedrick Smith's book have been insulated from many of the deficiencies of the consumer sector by special stores, but the great majority of the broad elite are becoming increasingly frustrated by the continuing shortages of consumer goods and services. Especially as the improvement in their own living standards has been lower than the average because of the twenty-five-year-old policy of greater wage equality, they have every reason to believe that greater wage differentials are vital to the economy.

Finally, within the top leadership itself, there must be a generational difference in the attitude toward economic reform, if for no other reason than the leadership energy it would demand. Brezhnev's speech to the November 1978 plenary session of the Central Committee, which was quoted near the beginning of this chapter, could hardly have been more negative about the performance of the economy had it been written by a Western critic of the Soviet system. His demand for economic reform and for an improvement in the consumer sector could scarcely have been more urgent, and, as has been seen, it was made on the grounds of political stability as well as of economic well-being. But the decision on economic reform that finally emerged in August 1979 was extremely general, and in some respects it even strengthened the central control of Gosplan. In practice, it had very little effect.[16]

Why was there such a contrast between the urgency of the Brezhnev speech and the rather meaningless decision that followed? Several explanations could be offered, but the most likely one is that the top leadership simply could not bring itself to pay the personal costs of significant economic reform. Whatever the various philosophical, economic, and political arguments that can be advanced for and against reform, it should never be forgotten that reform is burdensome and even painful to the leadership. A large number of institutional conflicts must be resolved at the beginning; a series of unexpected small and large difficulties, which will require authoritative decisions, are certain to arise almost continuously; and quite a few older administrative officials— many of them long-time personal friends of the leaders—will not function well in the new conditions and will need to be replaced. Even if everything works out very well, the work load for some of the top officials will be great, and if real problems emerge it will be immense.

It is most unlikely that Brezhnev's health would permit him to preside personally over the enactment of serious economic reform. Thus far he has shown no willingness to delegate such enormous power to one of his lieutenants. A healthier and more vigorous leader might well have a very different perspective. He might welcome the opportunity to exercise authority. Even more, he might be eager to remove the old friends of the former leaders among the top administrative elite and appoint men who would be politically loyal to him.

One should certainly not expect a new Soviet leader to institute

16. *Ekonomicheskaia gazeta*, no. 32 (August 1979), special supplement.

Yugoslavian market socialism in the near future, let alone to reestablish capitalism. But from the Western point of view, what would be of critical importance would be the willingness of a new leadership to adopt a favorable attitude toward economic reform and to take steps, if world conditions permitted, to expose the Soviet economy more to world market forces and to reduce the priority given to military expenditures. Such steps might not transform the Soviet economy, but they could, if the West were willing to respond, provide the basis for a relationship with the West that is far less dangerous than the events of the last few years seem to foretell.

8

Generational Change at the Top

NORMAL personnel turnover has unquestionably been occurring in the Soviet Union at levels just below the top. In one political and administrative hierarchy after another, as previous chapters have shown, there are second-level officials who are in the prime of life by Western standards. Regional party first secretaries averaged fifty-five years of age in early 1980, the other members of the RSFSR regional party bureaus were fifty-two, the commanders of the military districts were fifty-five, the heads of the desks in the Ministry of Foreign Affairs fifty-seven, and the directors of large industrial plants fifty.

Yet the situation at the very top has remained quite different. The inner ruling four—Brezhnev, Kosygin, Suslov, and Kirilenko—averaged seventy-five years of age in early 1980, and the other voting members of the Politburo averaged sixty-nine. The deputy chairmen of the Council of Ministers averaged sixty-seven, and the ministers and other members of the government not much younger (sixty-five). Even the regional first secretaries who held full membership in the Central Committee averaged fifty-nine, seven years older than the first secretaries who were not voting members.

In principle, with the departure of Brezhnev the stage is finally set for the disappearance of his generation from the political scene and for simultaneous major generational change at the ministerial level. Within a few years of its establishment, and perhaps sooner, the post-Brezhnev regime should have a general secretary of the 1910–18 generation (or, conceivably, younger), a Politburo composed of members of all three post-Brezhnev generations, ministers drawn from the wartime and postwar generations, and regional officials mainly from the postwar generation. Indeed, if the experience of the Stalin and Khrushchev regimes were to be repeated and the new general secretary preferred (and was able) to surround himself with men a decade younger, one would expect that within four or five years the Politburo members would come predominantly from the postwar generation.

It is easy to make such statements and to argue convincingly that

such developments in the realm of personnel policy are of critical importance for the vitality and perhaps even the stability of the system.
But to assert that something should or must occur is not to prove that it
will occur. People involved in a struggle for leadership posts are first of
all concerned about their personal interests, and the mechanisms of selection may provide the opportunity for a person or group to emerge
who is not ideal from the standpoint of the system as a whole.

Thoughts about the Succession

Because the timing of the succession is so uncertain and the age of
Politburo members so high, there is no reliable way to predict which
man will succeed Brezhnev or even which members will still be alive
and in good health when he is gone. But even if Westerners knew who
the next general secretary would be, the information would be of little
use. There is almost no Politburo figure of the Brezhnev period whose
position in the Soviet political spectrum has been agreed upon by
Western specialists.

Even consensus on the Aesopian implications of published speeches
of Politburo members might be of little help. Early in the 1920s it was
predicted that Stalin would be Lenin's successor, and the published
political discussion at the time was free enough to give most observers
a fairly clear impression that Stalin was one of the moderate, mediating
forces within the Politburo. Observers had much less information
about the situation in 1952–53 and 1963–64, but two of Stalin's top lieutenants in 1952 were Malenkov and Khrushchev (the third was the secret police head, Lavrentii Beria), and Khrushchev's two top deputies
in 1964 were Brezhnev and Kosygin. It is very difficult to believe that
the old leaders really understood how disenchanted the younger ones
were with the policies being followed. If Soviet leaders apparently cannot be certain about one another's views, outsiders should not expect
to be.

The most useful contribution that can be made beforehand to an understanding of the succession is to analyze the problems inherent in
this particular succession and the most likely possible variants—both
"healthy" and "pathological." In that way, as developments unfold,
we in America may have a clearer sense of their significance. Even
more important, we will have a sense of the range of possibilities and

may not blunder into policies that strengthen the probability of the variants most unfavorable to us. Such an approach may be especially valuable in the present case, for some unique problems exist that must be solved if the generational bottleneck in high-level personnel is to be overcome and policy unfrozen.

The first peculiarity of the next succession is that the age difference between the general secretary and other voting members of the Politburo is much narrower than in past successions. Stalin was seventy-three when he died and Khrushchev seventy when he was removed, but most of the other Politburo members of the time were ten to fifteen years younger. Generational change in the leadership was virtually inevitable whatever happened. But if Brezhnev had died in early 1980, at the age of seventy-three, seven of the thirteen remaining voting members of the Politburo would have been seventy years of age or older. Another four would have been between sixty-five and seventy.

Unless some unexpected crisis occurs, the selection of a new leader will be made through the regularized, legal mechanisms established for this purpose. The country's cabinet—the Politburo—will try to present an acceptable leadership slate to the institution that has the legal authority to take action, the Central Committee. The aging Politburo members have shown little inclination to retire, and it is far from clear that they will voluntarily advance a candidate who is dedicated to retiring them.

The second peculiarity of the next succession in light of the "lessons" of the three previous successions (admittedly a chancy exercise, given the very small number of them) is the absence of a logical successor in the present Politburo. In the earlier cases the new leader was the man in the Politburo with the broadest range of experience, and in particular the member with the greatest experience in dealing with the non-Russian population. Furthermore, he was the Politburo member with the best political base. Specifically, the victor in the succession struggle was the man who had been the old leader's chief lieutenant for supervision of the lower party apparatus. Conceivably this may have been simply a coincidence. The lower party organs are located in all areas of the country and have very diverse problems. Since the old leader naturally chose a man to supervise them who had a broad background in dealing with non-Russians as well as Russians, with agricultural as well as industrial problems, it may be the background of the official rather than the post that was the most important factor in the succession. Certainly in the smaller and less diversified countries of Eastern Europe, where this post is less demanding, its occupant is chosen less frequently as the successor.[1]

Western scholars, however, have emphasized the importance of the post of the man supervising the lower party apparatus rather than the breadth of his background. The choice of the general secretary and the Politburo members must be approved by the Central Committee. The membership of the Central Committee in turn is chosen or ratified by the party congresses. Although in theory the delegates to the congresses are elected democratically, they are chosen at regional party conferences, where the regional party secretaries have dominated the respective slates of delegates. The general secretary's main source of political strength has been the key role of the Secretariat in supervising the lower party apparatus. Because this responsibility implies the ability to remove ineffective lower officials and to select new ones, the general secretary—certainly under Stalin and Khrushchev, and apparently also under Brezhnev—has had control over the regional first secretaries. Not unnaturally, political loyalty becomes an important factor in the selection process, and the general secretary has been in a position to build a political machine.

But as the general secretary consolidates his position, he naturally wants to use his power to dominate the policy process. Consequently, he has far less time to supervise the lower party apparatus. The chief lieutenant whom he chooses for this activity may be able to select men who are loyal to him as well as to (or, perhaps, instead of to) the general secretary. Even if considerations of loyalty are not an explicit factor in personnel selection, the official overseeing the lower party organs at least knows lower officials and has not removed them; they in turn may believe that their chances with him are much better than with someone who does not know them.

Since 1966 Brezhnev's chief assistant for personnel selection has been Andrei Kirilenko. Kirilenko has had a reasonably wide range of experience in urban areas, including those in the Ukraine and Russian republics. But, unlike his predecessors, he is not the general secretary's junior. Kirilenko was born in 1906, the same year as Brezhnev,

1. Myron Rush, *How Communist States Change Their Rulers* (Cornell University Press, 1974), pp.295-98.

and had his first lengthy contact with his future boss in the position of an equal, or perhaps even a superior, in the first year of the war.[2] After the war Brezhnev became first secretary of the Zaporozhe regional party committee and Kirilenko the second secretary. Kirilenko's fortunes rose thereafter with Brezhnev's, but despite his continuing subordinate position, Kirilenko was always a colleague. When Politburo members reach their seventieth birthday, they receive a medal in a public meeting and exchange short speeches with Brezhnev. Of all the Politburo members, Kirilenko was the only one who felt able to refer to Brezhnev in the familiar form of "you"—"*ty*"—in this public forum.[3]

Thus a Kirilenko succession in 1980 would mean a new leader of seventy-three and one with little independent identity. As of mid-1980, no man below the age of seventy holds another post in the central party or governmental apparatus that seems to provide a good base of power for the succession. No doubt, this fact is not accidental, but instead reflects a conscious Brezhnev policy of trying to prevent a premature succession—that is, of avoiding someone doing to him what he had done to Khrushchev in 1964. But if there is no "logical" successor in terms of normal criteria of selection, the problem of which "illogical" candidate might be chosen is next to impossible to determine by anyone with as little information as is available in the West.

In mid-1980 a variety of succession patterns seem possible. The successor himself could come from the Brezhnev generation (almost surely Kirilenko), from the 1910–18 generation (probably Victor Grishin or Vladimir Shcherbitsky), or even from the wartime or postwar generation (the likeliest candidate being Georgii Romanov or Mikhail Gorbachev).

In many ways the most important question about the Soviet future is the fate of the Politburo members other than Brezhnev in the wake of the succession. After Khrushchev's removal in 1964, few other Politburo members were replaced for the next eight years, and even after

2. Kirilenko spent five months in late 1941 and early 1942 as "member of the military council" of the Eighteenth Army—the top political officer in that army. At first, Brezhnev was the deputy head of the political administration (the number-three political officer) of the South Front under which the Eighteenth Army served, a post more or less equal to Kirilenko's. In 1942 Brezhnev became head of the political administration of the Eighteenth Army—the number-two political officer in it—but it is unclear whether Kirilenko was still there and served as Brezhnev's boss or whether he had moved on.

3. *Pravda*, October 15, 1976, pp. 1–2.

Lenin's and Stalin's deaths the process of Politburo renewal took approximately five years. If such is the case in the post-Brezhnev succession, the probability of significant change in the near or medium term does not seem too high. It is unlikely that a Politburo majority in their seventies would want to change policies with which they had worked for fifteen years or that they would have the energy to do so.

Yet it is possible to imagine a pattern of Politburo replacement quite different from that in the past. Half or more of the members of the Politburo could easily be retired within a year of the succession, some of the principal ones at the time of the succession itself. If this were to happen, a new leader—or a new inner circle of leaders—would almost surely try to present the image of a dynamic leadership seeking change. Not only would such a policy help to establish his authority, but it would give him the opportunity to replace many central governmental and party officials and to build his own political machine.

In 1964 Brzezinski and Samuel P. Huntington described a close relationship between the policy process and the process of acquiring power:

Policies—foreign and domestic—are major weapons in the struggle for power within the system. . . . During a succession crisis, each leadership faction appeals for support to different institutional groups; each attempts to endow its policy with ideological legitimacy; and each strives to demonstrate the opponents' deviationism. . . . Competition for power in the Soviet Union tends to magnify policy differences between the contestants.[4]

Although this kind of phenomenon was not evident during the Brezhnev period, the reasons for the analysis have not vanished, and it could accurately describe the strategy that the next leader will follow.

The second set of questions about the succession regards the circumstances under which it takes place. In retrospect, the best way to have predicted the direction of policy change in previous successions would have been to have tried to get some sense of the dominant mood within the party as a whole. In the late 1920s the party members consisted largely of workers and peasants who had been admitted in the previous few years and who may have begun to rise into low-level political and administrative work. On balance, they seemed uneasy about the retreat from socialist transformation, especially since it was ac-

4. Zbigniew Brzezinski and Samuel P. Huntington, *Political Power: USA/USSR* (Viking, 1964) pp. 191–93.

companied by an increase in unemployment. In the early 1950s many party members were surely yearning for relief from the terror and from the policy stagnation of the late Stalin period. And after a dozen years of Khrushchev's reorganizations and experiments, they were undoubtedly anxious for more stability. In each of these periods, the new leader went further—probably much further—than the party would have desired, but at least he aligned himself with major social forces; to varying degrees his selection may have depended on that fact.

In an age in which all the leading politicians have risen slowly through bureaucratic hierarchies, it would be natural for any new leader to try to solidify his position in a similar way rather than to risk loss of support by challenging influential interests. It is for this reason that the kind of generational change discussed in this book has the potential to be so important. Although the views of any one man can differ greatly from the average opinions of members of his generation, a generational change within an entire political and administrative elite can affect the flow of advice significantly. A change in leader—and in the personal staff and cabinet of a leader—can mean that the flow of advice may have a different impact, especially if the old leader had grown increasingly resistant to innovation.

Despite the inherent difficulties in judging the mood within the party as a whole, much impressionistic evidence does suggest growing dissatisfaction with the mix of policy in the Brezhnev era. The general secretary's 1978 speech to the Central Committee expressed a widespread and growing dissatisfaction with the economic performance in consumer goods and services, and, as mentioned before, he himself alluded to the political dangers that shortages were creating. Although in the West Brezhnev has the reputation of being a dove, he has had close ties with the military throughout his career. It is likely that he has been one of the Politburo hard-liners pushing a steady rise in military expenditures and resisting arms control. Because extensive dissatisfaction with the level of Soviet military expenditures clearly exists, others would conceivably be more willing to take stronger initiatives to try to reduce it.

Among the educated and the skilled in particular (and, to repeat, over half the male college graduates eventually become party members), there must be real unhappiness with the continuing Brezhnev policy of increasing wage equality—that is, of giving larger percentage income increases to workers and peasants than to members of the managerial elite. In his November 1978 speech Brezhnev also denounced the quality of the press reporting on international affairs. This complaint, too, surely reflects the increasing impatience of the educated with the tightness of the censorship, the sterility of much of the ideological phrasemongering, and the limitations on contact with the West. The manner in which the Afghanistan story was reported in the Soviet press—the patently improbable claim that the USSR had been invited to invade and the subsequent failure to report military actions—can only increase this feeling.

Above all, there must be a profound sense of the tiredness of the Brezhnev regime and a desire to get the country moving again, whatever the direction, a desire often coupled with a feeling that younger men should get a chance. Since a number of factors militate against the attractiveness of a multiparty constitutional democracy for the Soviet (and especially the Russian) attentive public, the line of development that seems the most attractive—and, therefore, perhaps most likely—is an attempt at greater liberalization, economic reform, and income differentiation (in the name of increasing incentives), more or less on the Hungarian model.

A political succession that takes place in the wake of a crisis, however, will have a different set of social forces to which to respond—forces that, even if temporary, may be powerful. If, for example, a critical situation developed between the Soviet Union and the United States in the Middle East, the Soviet political system would require a leader who could work fifteen hours a day and who could take decisive actions based on a careful weighing of many factors. In such circumstances the Central Committee might well demand a much younger leader than Brezhnev and one with strong policy views. The direction of his policy orientation would reflect the immediate needs of the time as seen by the Central Committee rather than the impact of long-term considerations.

American Foreign Policy and the Soviet Future

Over the years Soviet studies in the United States has been absorbed with the problem of prediction. Even many of our scholarly models are concerned not with the functioning of the contemporary system, but with the presumed direction of its evolution. Governmental political research on the Soviet Union is also focused on prediction, but prediction of a narrow type: who will be the successor and what will be his characteristics?

It is highly doubtful whether prediction should occupy so central a place in our work and thinking. First, our predictions have been so consistently wrong that this alone should discourage us. Second, the Soviet future is probably not predetermined—or at least in any way that we can know. Third—and most important—one of the factors that will influence the direction of Soviet society is the changing nature of the outside environment, and we are part of that environment. Instead of engaging in abstract forecasting that ignores our own part in the process, we would be better advised to try to understand the impact of that environment and, above all, the ways in which we can affect it.

To a great extent, this way of thinking tends to be foreign to us. The process of socializing a constant stream of immigrants into American culture, of inculcating the political values of the system into them, and of creating a sense of common national identity has made the U.S. system strongly ideological in many respects, especially when the fundamentals of national identity and of the system become involved. One result has been, as many observers have noted, a heavy streak of moralism, messianism, unconscious arrogance, and self-righteousness in American foreign policy. In any unpleasant international situation it becomes difficult for us to see a neutral clash of interests, let alone the possibility that the other side may be reacting to behavior on our part that might be considered unacceptable by international standards. We therefore have a strong tendency to see any unfavorable foreign policy actions by others as stemming from unworthy inner drives. This reduces our sense of being able to influence their behavior by methods other than military resistance. The problem is particularly great in our relationship with the Soviet Union because of our propensity to see that country in abstract terms, as being driven by some inner logic.

In practice, however, the nature of the Soviet leadership matters to us. In the first place, nuclear weapons have had an impact on the theory of deterrence that is unappreciated beyond a narrow circle of international relations theorists. In the past, establishing deterrence involved the building of sufficient forces and the assembling of a powerful enough alliance to make a potential aggressor feel that an attack would not succeed. The calculations that were necessary were relatively simple estimates of actual and potential divisions, weapons, and the like, although, of course, many wars of this century followed fundamental miscalculations on the part of the expansionist powers.

In a nuclear age the problem of calculation is qualitatively different. Assuming that each side has the ability to devastate the other, it is irrational for either one to attack or defend unless its fundamental interests are at stake. For example, if the result will be the destruction of the principal Soviet cities, it cannot be a rational calculation for the Soviet Union to seize Berlin or northern Iran, even if the Soviet Union could wipe out American cities in response to American nuclear retaliation. Conversely, if the result will be the destruction of the principal American cities, it cannot be rational for the United States to launch a nuclear attack on the Soviet Union as a response to a Soviet seizure of Berlin or northern Iran. The same set of calculations apply, although in reverse, to a hypothetical American effort to invade Cuba. So if the defensive side can trust the rationality of the potential aggressor, a convincing threat of nuclear retaliation—that is, a pledge to act irrationally—will defer a conventional attack. At the same time, if the aggressor can trust the rationality of the defender, it is perfectly safe for it to launch a conventional attack, so long as it has the preponderance of conventional force in a given case.

In short, nuclear deterrence is analogous to the teenagers' game of chicken in which two drivers speed toward each other, each with the left wheel of his car on the yellow line in the middle of the road. A rational driver in this game will always veer away at the last moment, for the taunt of being a coward is not as bad as death. Therefore, if one can count upon one's opponent to be rational, it is safe to keep driving straight ahead. If each driver is convinced of the other's rationality, disaster occurs.

In these circumstances, deterrence is not just a matter of accumulating more rockets or making additional threats. Nothing we can do will change the fact that the United States is approximately thirty minutes from nuclear destruction and that only the rationality and the caution of the Soviet leaders stand between us and that destruction. Our military posture will be an important factor in instilling a sense of caution in the Soviet Union, but we should never forget that another factor in deterrence is a leadership on the other side that is essentially balanced and rational and that is in a position to act in a balanced and rational manner. If the leaders on either side or both sides encourage games of chicken or engage in brinkmanship, if they repeatedly make direct challenges to the manhood of the opponent, the probability increases that the situation will get out of control.

In the second place, the nature of the Soviet leadership matters to us because the policy choices that the Soviet leaders must make in the early 1980s matter to us. A decision to conduct economic reform based on greater integration of the Soviet Union into the world economy and on an attempt to control military expansion and even reduce the size of the army would relieve our economic and military problems. At a time when rapidly rising fuel prices are draining American resources abroad and placing limits on a rise or even a maintenance of the consumption level of the population and when a consensus is growing that too small a part of GNP is going to investment, military expenditures and military consumption of petroleum clearly create a greater burden on the economy than they did in the past.

By contrast, a Soviet leadership that promotes a jingoistic foreign policy, expands the military, and tries to operate an autarkic economy in which real pressure is exerted on consumption is scarcely in our interest. Even aside from the direct threats to our welfare that such a policy would entail, we would continually find ourselves in a position where the sanctions we might apply (for example, the prohibition of the sale of oil drills) are as harmful to us as to them.

With a succession crisis—or crises—imminent in which there seems to be no clear-cut or even logical successor, it is obviously in our interest to try to encourage the Soviet elite to select a leader dedicated to the restoration of détente. And whatever new leader is selected, it is obviously in our interest to try to encourage him to act in a more conciliatory way.

But how do we achieve these goals? In principle, the answer is fairly straightforward. We should try to influence the incentive system in which the Soviet elite and, later, the new Soviet leader operate. We should use a combination of carrot and stick that promises the Soviet Union some advantage if it follows a more accommodating policy and threatens it with real penalties if its policy is unsatisfactory. That is, we should try to affect the costs and benefits for the Soviet Union in a way that would produce a more favorable outcome in any rational Soviet cost-benefit analysis. We should have a clear sense of the priority of our interests, as well as of the benefits that we might reasonably expect to achieve for ourselves without paying more than they are worth.

Such a statement is quite unexceptional at the theoretical level, but it does not correspond to the way we have thought about Soviet-American relations, especially in the last few years.

First, we as a nation have not decided what we can reasonably hope from the Soviet Union as a nation and what our policy can achieve. Verbally, we recognize the Soviet Union as a Great Power—even as an equal—but then we become upset when it begins to act like an equal. Many people in the United States—including many who see themselves as hard-line realists—view détente in much the same way as Cordell Hull pictured international relations of the future. In this view, détente seems to mean a world without conflicts of interest among the superpowers. Or, rather, it implies a world in which the United States is free to pursue its interests, but in which the Soviet Union cannot pursue its own without breaking the code of détente. It is legitimate for the United States to support the transportation of Moroccan troops to Zaire, but not for the Soviet Union to support Cuban troops in Ethiopia. It is legitimate for the United States to organize the financing of non-Communist forces in Portugal and to try to arrange congenial governments in Nicaragua and Zimbabwe, but it is illegitimate for the Soviet Union to support the forces in those countries that are friendly to it.

That we should attempt to counter Soviet behavior that is contrary to our interests is natural, but instead of merely defending these interests, we have had a strong tendency to become morally outraged when they are challenged. As a result we often lose our sense of proportion and priority and weaken our ability to defend interests that are of the greatest importance to us. The Soviet suppression of a dissident like Anatolii Shcharansky or our discovery of a few thousand troops in Cuba produces such a strong response and atmosphere of crisis that we reduce the leverage available to us to deter an invasion of Afghanistan. In turn, our response to that invasion left us with few additional measures to take short of nuclear war if the Soviet Union were to take some further step.

Second, we have fallen into the pattern of reacting to the Soviet Union—really, of punishing it—rather than of seeking to deter it. So far as one can judge, the Soviet Union was genuinely surprised that the invasion of Afghanistan provoked a grain embargo and a policy of boycotting the Olympics. Whatever the arguments that may arise about the wisdom of these steps, it was surely a great mistake to have forsworn the grain weapon publicly instead of making it clear beforehand that this was a potential cost the Soviet leadership should be weighing. Similarly, in the wake of the Afghanistan invasion, discussion has centered far more on how to hurt the Soviet Union for this misdeed instead of on how to prevent misdeeds in the future.

If we are going to influence the Soviet cost-benefit calculations effectively in the 1980s, we need to be able to evaluate the costs and benefits that we are asking the Soviet leaders to choose between, and we need to increase the gap between them. In the second half of the 1970s, the United States—first and foremost, the Congress, but also the administration—fell into the habit of describing as intolerable Soviet behavior quite similar to that in which we engage and then blustering in a threatening manner without being willing to provide incentives or sanctions to support our words.

Our greatest problem has been an exaggerated sense of the importance of the costs and benefits we usually discuss. Many Americans talk as if selling a computer to the Soviet Union is an enormous benefit for that country or as if refusing to ratify SALT or encouraging the sale of arms to mainland China is an inordinately high cost. Yet with the Soviet economy approaching the trillion dollar level, an American decision to grant or deny a trade deal worth a million dollars really has no significant impact. Similarly, SALT has been so permissive in its limits on the military of the two countries that the threat of nonratification cannot be very frightening.

The most dangerous leverage at our disposal is "the China card." The establishment of U.S. diplomatic and commercial relations with China is desirable from all points of view, but strong verbal support of China in its conflict with the Soviet Union and especially the provision of military aid are very sensitive matters that rub salt in the rawest Soviet wound. Although the China card can for this reason sometimes be effective, it is dangerous because we are not in a position to seriously affect the military balance between the Soviet Union and China for years to come. Thus we can irritate the Soviet Union by our military dealing with China without directly reducing its military freedom of action vis-à-vis China. A provocative policy without the power to back it up courts humiliation or worse.

Instead of selling or withholding an occasional computer, we should be offering a comprehensive American-Japanese program to assist in the development of Soviet oil fields along with our threats to end grain sales. Instead of taking years over a largely cosmetic SALT II treaty, we should be coupling our threats to increase military spending 5 percent a year with proposals for large reductions in conventional and strategic forces. Instead of simply irritating the Soviet Union with meaningless gestures toward China, we should encourage China to devote its meager resources to the industrial development that will in the long run permit it to serve as a counterweight to the Soviet Union. We should make clear to everyone that our interests in having access to Middle East oil are as great as were our interests in Europe in 1917 and 1941, and that we will use all conceivable weapons to defend them.

Above all, we should adopt the posture of a confident and mature Great Power dealing with an equal. It does not contribute to an image of strength to become overconcerned about 2,000 Soviet troops in Cuba. Even less does it contribute to an image of confidence to act as if history were moving inexorably against us in the third world and as if a relatively small number of Cuban troops would be able to conquer the African continent. And it is sheer idiocy to discuss the "vulnerability" of our Minutemen in a way that suggests that we might submit to a massive nuclear attack on the continental United States—with all the fallout involved—without retaliating in kind.

Of course, we need to understand that no matter how skillful our diplomacy, no matter how resolute our will, events will occur that are unpleasant from our point of view. The Soviet Union is a Great Power; it has interests that conflict with our own; the legitimacy of its political system is strengthened by developments in the outside world that are quite different from those that strengthen the legitimacy of our political system. Like the United States, the Soviet Union, which perceives itself as an equal, is going to try to influence developments in directions favorable to it.

Indeed, results that we do not like will occur regardless of the wishes and policies of the Soviet Union. The third world has long been basically anti-Western and pro-socialist in its rhetoric, and most third world countries have long supported the Soviet Union on many votes in the United Nations. Lenin's theory of imperialism is enormously attractive in those areas, where the idea of the inherently exploitative nature of Western policy fits well with preexisting preconceptions and grievances and provides third world politicians with a good excuse for the existence of economic problems that might otherwise be blamed on them. Moreover, in countries with few native industrialists and little capital, it is natural for young college graduates to want to enter governmental work and to have government play a dominant role in economic development and equally natural for them to adopt ideologies that legitimate that role.

Although our politicians and media tend to treat the third world as our sphere of influence and see any increase in Soviet influence as an intolerable loss of what is inherently ours, the nature of the third world is such that it will never move en masse to the side of any one Great Power. There are too many external and internal checks and balances for that to occur. Innumerable local conflicts like that between Somalia and Ethiopia will push the two local rivals to seek the support of competing Great Powers. Similarly, a regime that is uncertain of its popular support may decide to link itself with one of the superpowers in an attempt to get economic and military aid, but when that occurs, its political enemies will naturally rally against it under the banner of national independence. And given the strength of nationalism and the degree of political instability in the third world, these enemies are quite likely to be successful over time. Also, of course, if one superpower— especially the Soviet Union—becomes too successful, that too will create fears and cause a reaction. Soviet suppression of Moslems in Afghanistan, for example, must create strong pressures on leaders in the Middle East to seek American protection as the lesser evil.

Because of the political instability and because of the number of countries in the third world, it seems natural that in almost any year a few countries would be in the process of changing their position in the Soviet-American competition. The problem for both the United States and the Soviet Union is to learn to treat these developments with some perspective. Americans must break the pattern of seeing any Soviet gain as calamitous and irreversible, while perversely paying almost no attention to our gains. (One wonders how many Americans are aware that a Marxist-Leninist regime was overthrown in Equatorial Guinea in 1979 or that Idi Amin, the former president of Uganda, had flirted with the Soviet Union.)

Some Soviet scholars argue that in most third world countries there are powerful forces working against continued socialistic development over the medium term. They regard foreign investment as essential for countries without substantial oil revenue, because of the scarcity of internal capital and the limited amount of Soviet foreign aid available. They also believe that retail trade and cottage industry must remain private if the economy is to function effectively. As a result, officials in the governmental sector have an opportunity to accumulate funds through bribery and other forms of corruption and to funnel them into the private sector, perhaps through relatives. Soon, the Soviet scholars fear, the officials stop supporting socialism and begin to form a capitalist class, with all its characteristic attitudes. This analysis may be too pessimistic from the Soviet point of view and too optimistic from the American, but it is surely relevant. The signs of change in Angola, Iraq, Mozambique, Yemen, and Zimbabwe during the last year suggest that it may often be valid.

It is, of course, one thing to say that the natural forces at work in the third world will lead to a series of shifting political outcomes, but another to say that natural forces will be allowed to work. Since World War II the Soviet Union has acted as if the preservation of the Marxist-Leninist regimes in East Europe were of such vital interest that it would use troops to maintain them in power. It was successful in distancing itself from such so-called socialist allies as Gamal Abdel Nasser of Egypt and Kwame Nkrumah of Ghana, but in recent years a number of leftist leaders in the third world countries have proclaimed themselves Marxist-Leninists, and they pose a real problem. Suspicious that such self-proclamations may be little more than attempts to win economic and military support and afraid that its prestige may become too closely tied to a series of unstable regimes, the Soviet Union has declared that these "Marxist-Leninist" governments (except for those in Cuba and Vietnam) fit within the "socialist-orientation" category rather than the socialist one. However, if the Soviet Union becomes convinced that its prestige depends on the irreversibility of these Marxist-Leninist revolutions in the third world and that it should or must intervene militarily if they are near collapse, the situation becomes dangerous. The Soviet leaders may have thought that because Afghanistan had been in the Soviet sphere of influence for decades it was a special case. But the invasion of Afghanistan has set a precedent that, if followed, will ultimately lead to World War III.

American Foreign Policy and Soviet Generational Change

The argument that a country should think of foreign policy in cost-benefit terms and that it should have a clear idea of the priority of its interests and the limits of what it can achieve obviously applies to foreign relations between any countries and at any time. The fact that generational change may be imminent in the Soviet Union does not alter these basic principles, but it does increase the urgency that they be followed.

In the first place, with the Soviet Union facing critical choices in the early 1980s—choices that will probably be made only by a new leadership—it is vital that we offer some hope that it can pursue a policy of economic reform, liberalization, and reduction of military expenditures without national humiliation. The Soviet leaders have hungered for equality with the West since the 1920s, and have driven their people to enormous sacrifices to achieve it. The Russian people have acquiesced in party rule largely because the party has successfully identified itself with the values of national dignity and power; neither the people nor the elite will respond well to a leadership that is perceived to be abandoning that goal because of foreign pressure. Certainly it is impossible to believe that any leadership will abandon it. If the Soviet leaders assume that the United States will not permit reductions in its military expenditures, if they are convinced that any attempt to advance Soviet interests (even by means the United States habitually uses in defending its interests) will foreclose trade and arms control with the United States, the policy choices they make are likely to be as unpleasant for us as they are for the Soviet people.

In the second place, a generational change within the Politburo—regardless of the policy perspectives of the new leaders—is likely to bring about a more activist and innovative foreign policy. Except for the use of Cuban troops in Africa (which Soviet scholars insist was the result of Cuban initiative), Brezhnev's foreign policy has been reactive, in stereotyped ways. The Soviet Union has consistently supported anti-American forces in its propaganda (even when, as in Iran, propagandistic support of Ayatollah Khomeini is probably not in Soviet domestic interests); it has fought rearmament of Western Europe with the tactics of the old peace movements of the 1940s rather than through willingness to bargain away its rocket and conventional forces in East Europe; it has stubbornly held onto four worthless islands when all geopolitical and economic considerations dictated a need to court Japan vigorously; it used an invasion to preserve its position in Afghanistan when a KGB coup would surely have been more in its interests. The Soviet leaders responded well to Henry Kissinger's subtle diplomacy and angrily to Brzezinski's goading, but they themselves never seem to have thought to use Kissinger-like tactics on the United States.

A new and younger leadership is likely to be more self-confident in its international actions. It may be more willing to take risks for diplomatic gains (for example, in regard to the four islands near Japan), to promote arms control by sacrificing old weapons, to engage in quiet diplomacy that helps to overcome domestic political problems on both sides. Or it may be more willing to take risks involving military action. But in either case the penalties that we are likely to incur by failing to influence Soviet cost-benefit calculations may be much more severe than they have been in the Brezhnev era.

In the third place, although the postwar generation of officials is, of course, divided in its views, on balance it should have different priorities from those of the generation whose whole life was associated with the great Soviet industrialization drive and the policy of catching up with the West militarily. The younger officials are determined to have the Soviet Union treated as an equal, but they are more secure in taking that equality for granted. They certainly feel that they have the right to support "progressive" forces around the world—human rights in a Marxist-Leninist perspective, if you will—but the West is a source of attraction as much as a source of encirclement and danger. Above all, they seem eager to move from the Marxist-based social programs of egalitarianism of Khrushchev and Brezhnev to an era emphasizing economic growth and consumerism, especially since a policy of greater incentives means greater power and income for themselves.

It is for us to give this new generation of officials the opportunity, the excuse, to move in the direction that its instincts are pushing it. If we demand that the Soviet Union renounce the right to act as a world power, we are going to be disappointed. If we demand that it abstain from action in the third world that we take for granted for ourselves, we are going to be just as disappointed. Moreover, if we deeply offend the Soviet sense of dignity and equality and issue ultimatums on types of behavior that we are not willing to forswear ourselves, we will indeed run serious risks.

Our first priority should be to try to assure the Soviet Union that reduction of military expenditures is a workable option, and this in turn requires us to regard economy in the military realm as a positive good. Frequently those within both the defense and the arms-control communities become so absorbed in the games of achieving either advantage or "stability" that cost is forgotten. There may be countervailing factors that must be dominant at a time when Soviet troops have invaded Afghanistan, but in principle we must learn to think of increased Soviet or Chinese petroleum production as a plus, of increased petroleum consumption by Soviet, Chinese, American—or other— tanks as a minus. We need to understand that a partial Soviet-Chinese reconciliation that resulted in a reduction in the size of the Soviet army would be more advantageous to us than the present level of Soviet-Chinese enmity when China is so weak. We need to try not only to influence Soviet cost-benefit calculations but also to weigh our own choices more in these terms. We need to ask whether expenditures on yet another strategic rocket or bomber add as much to the potential defense of our real interests as a conventional force that is deployable in the Middle East and to ask whether we can afford both.

Our second priority must be to convey to a Soviet elite choosing a new leader— or to the new leader himself—the sense that we are a mature and confident power, determined to protect our vital interests and our people's well-being pragmatically, willing both to compete and to cooperate when it serves our interests. We should show that we no more fear Soviet verbal support of third world revolution than we fear to give verbal support to third world democrats or democrats in the Soviet Union like Andrei Sakharov. We should show as much disdain for small Soviet brigades in Cuba as they show for small American forces in Turkey. A Great Power's willingness to defend—even fight for—its vital interests need not be coupled with panic when minor interests are challenged or when minor losses are incurred.

As we compete with the Soviet Union in a mature manner, it will cost us little to treat the Soviet Union with dignity as an equal, and it may pay enormous benefits. When we speak of SALT or trade as a favor to the Soviet Union, when we fail to treat cooperation as something the United States needs as well as the Soviet Union, when we talk as if the Soviet Union were a third-rate power that had no business being interested in third world developments, we should at least understand that we are being deeply offensive without accomplishing anything. Even our criticism of the Soviet politico-social system would be easier to accept if we also said that ultimately it is for the Soviet people, not the American, to determine the future course of development of Soviet society.

But perhaps most of all we need to convince ourselves that change is possible—not the achievement of perfection, but improvement. We need to call repeatedly for reasonable change of a kind that we are willing to match, and we need to promise repeatedly to try to respond to change in Soviet behavior. The generational change that is imminent in the Soviet Union gives us reason to hope—not to be certain, but to hope. It gives us the opportunity to make limited-risk efforts, if we can act intelligently and maturely. If we can, perhaps future historians will point to generational change not in one country but in two, and perhaps they will be able to report that the 1980s saw significant adjustment in Great Power relations in response to the changing military and economic realities of the time. If not, the Soviet and American propensity for escalating the conflict that marked the late 1970s may lead to a situation in which there will be few historians able to report about the 1980s at all.

Index

Academy of Sciences, 43, 60, 105, 107, 121, 122, 124. *See also* Scholarly community
Administrative system, structure of, 5–6, 65–66, 71–72, 73, 137–38, 140–41. *See also* Agricultural administration; Industrial administration; Ministries; and Regional party organs
Afghanistan, 17, 126; Soviet invasion of, 1, 2, 157, 164, 165–66, 167; U.S. response to invasion of, 3, 161, 162, 168
Africa, 126, 161, 163, 166
Agricultural administration, 42–43, 52, 55, 56, 74
Aleksandrov-Agentov, Andrei M., 110, 111, 112, 113
Amin, Idi, 165
Andropov, Iurii V., 109, 111, 112, 113, 124
Angola, 165
Antonov, Aleksei I., 88
Arbatov, Georgii A., 124, 126
Arkhipov, Ivan V., 110, 111, 112
Armstrong, John A., 141
Arzumanian, Anushavan A., 121–22, 124
Attentive public, 23–25, 27–29

Bagramian, Ivan Kh., 88, 92n, 94n, 96n, 97n
Berg, Aksel I., 88n
Beriia, Lavrentii P., 151
Biriuzov, Sergei S., 96n
Blatov, Anatolii I., 110, 111, 113
Bovin, Alexander V., 124
Brazil, 17, 31
Brezhnev generation, 15, 40–48, 52, 58, 59, 69, 79, 80, 144, 154
Brezhnev, Leonid I., 109, 111; career, 46, 48, 65, 91, 92, 97–98, 143, 150, 151, 153–54; consolidation of power, 10, 72–73, 77, 152, 153, 154; policies, 4, 32–33, 35, 135, 151, 156–57; relationship with military, 91, 97–99, 156; speeches on economic reform, 11, 12, 14, 133–34, 138, 148; speech on media, 32–33
Brinton, Crane, 33, 35–36

Brutents, Karen N., 124
Brzezinski, Zbigniew, 4n, 14n, 155, 167
Budenny, Semen M., 81
Bulganin, Nikolai A., 87, 88, 91, 92, 93
Bureaucracy. *See* Administrative system
Burlatsky, Fedor M., 124

Central Committee, 62–64, 68, 75–77, 152, 153
Central Committee Secretariat and apparatus, 62, 68, 76–77, 153; characteristics of officials, 68–69, 70, 71, 73, 123–24, 126, 140–41
Chernenko, Konstantin U., 14, 62
China, 17, 168
China card, 162–63
Chuikov, Vasilii I., 92, 96n, 97n
Civil war, 5, 27–38, 40, 41, 81, 91
Colton, Timothy J., 90, 91
Comintern, 111, 112, 113, 117, 128
Communism, appeal of, 11, 16–18, 33–34, 136, 166–67
Communist party: apparatus, 27, 138–39, 140–41; membership, 6, 24–29, 33–34, 44, 49, 50–51, 155–56. *See also* Central Committee; Central Committee Secretariat and apparatus; Politburo; Primary party organizations; Regional party organs
Consumer goods sector, 14, 74, 131, 134, 137, 138, 147, 148, 156
Council of Ministers, 61, 63; deputy chairmen, 67–68, 70. *See also* Ministers
Cuba, 17, 159, 161, 163, 165, 166
Cultural revolution, 46, 49, 114

Daniels, Robert V., 77
Dekanozov, Vladimir, 114
Demichev, Peter N., 111n
Democratization, prospects of, 11, 12, 16–18, 29–30, 32–33, 34–36, 65, 157
Demographic problem of the 1980s, 11, 131, 132–33, 137, 147. *See also* Labor utilization
Deterrence theory, 158–60, 161–62